P9-DJU-969

Global Initiatives to Secure Cyberspace

An Emerging Landscape

Advances in Information Security

Sushil Jajodia

Consulting Editor
Center for Secure Information Systems
George Mason University
Fairfax, VA 22030-4444
email: jajodia@gmu.edu

The goals of the Springer International Series on ADVANCES IN INFORMATION SECURITY are, one, to establish the state of the art of, and set the course for future research in information security and, two, to serve as a central reference source for advanced and timely topics in information security research and development. The scope of this series includes all aspects of computer and network security and related areas such as fault tolerance and software assurance.

ADVANCES IN INFORMATION SECURITY aims to publish thorough and cohesive overviews of specific topics in information security, as well as works that are larger in scope or that contain more detailed background information than can be accommodated in shorter survey articles. The series also serves as a forum for topics that may not have reached a level of maturity to warrant a comprehensive textbook treatment.

Researchers, as well as developers, are encouraged to contact Professor Sushil Jajodia with ideas for books under this series.

Global Initiatives to Secure Cyberspace
An Emerging Landscape

Edited by

Michael Portnoy
Georgia Institute of Technology
Atlanta, GA, USA

Seymour Goodman
Georgia Institute of Technology
Atlanta, GA, USA

Contributors:

Michael Portnoy, Kathleen Minor, Andrew Howard,
William Lee, Richard Givens, Irene Liscano,
Delphine Nain, Seymour Goodman

 Springer

Editors:
Michael Portnoy
Georgia Institute of Technology
Georgia Tech Information Security Center
Sam Nunn School of Int'l Affairs
Center for International Strategy,
Technology, & Policy
781 Marietta St.
Atlanta GA 30332
mportnoy@gatech.edu

Seymour Goodman
Georgia Institute of Technology
Georgia Tech Information Security Center
Sam Nunn School of Int'l Affairs
Center for International Strategy,
Technology, & Policy
781 Marietta St.
Atlanta GA 30332
goodman@cc.gatech.edu

ISBN-13: 978-0-387-09763-3   e-ISBN-13: 978-0-387-09764-0

Library of Congress Control Number: 2008936298

© 2009 Springer Science+Business Media, LLC.
All rights reserved. This work may not be translated or copied in whole or in part
without the written permission of the publisher (Springer Science+Business Media,
LLC, 233 Spring Street, New York, NY 10013, USA), except for brief excerpts in
connection with reviews or scholarly analysis. Use in connection with any form of
information storage and retrieval, electronic adaptation, computer software, or by
similar or dissimilar methodology now known or hereafter developed is forbidden.
The use in this publication of trade names, trademarks, service marks and similar
terms, even if they are not identified as such, is not to be taken as an expression of
opinion as to whether or not they are subject to proprietary rights.

Printed on acid-free paper

springer.com

Preface

As cyberspace continues to rapidly expand, its infrastructure is now an integral part of the world's economy and social structure. Given this increasing interconnectivity and interdependence, what progress has been made in developing an ecosystem of safety and security? This study is the second phase of an initial attempt to survey and catalog the multitude of emerging organizations promoting global initiatives to secure cyberspace.

The authors provide a breakdown and analysis of organizations by type, including international, regional, private-public, and non-governmental organizations. Concluding with a discussion of the progress made in recent years, the study explores current trends regarding the effectiveness and scope of coverage provided by these organizations and addresses several questions concerning the overall state of international cyber security.

The authors would like to thank Mr. Anthony Rutkowski for generously providing his time, guidance, and support. The authors would also like to thank the International Telecommunication Union (ITU) Telecommunication Development Sector (ITU-D) and the United States National Science Foundation (NSF Grant R3772) for partially supporting the research conducted in this study. In addition, the authors would like to thank the Georgia Institute of Technology's Center for International Strategy, Technology, and Policy (CISTP) for assistance in hosting the Cyber Security Organization Catalog, and the Georgia Tech Information Security Center (GTISC) for cooperation and promotion of this study.

Table of Contents

1 The International Landscape of Cyber Security

Cyberspace – the "worldwide open IP-enabled network infrastructure for communications, commerce, and government" [1] – continues to expand rapidly. The average number of Internet users has increased an estimated 304 percent between 2000 and 2008 and is now quickly approaching 1.5 billion. The majority of relative growth has occurred in developing regions such as the Middle East, Africa, and Latin America, while close to half of the absolute growth has occurred in Asia. [2]

A function of this ever-increasing interconnectivity and interdependence, cyberspace has now become an integral part of the world's economy and social structure. Individuals, industry, and government all rely on information and communication technologies (ICTs) for a wide variety of needs, such as banking, electric power, emergency services, transportation, education, telecommunication, social networking, military operations, and critical infrastructure control. [3]

However, this substantial growth in cyberspace usage has not been accompanied by an adequate increase in security. In the nascent days of the Advanced Research Projects Agency Network (ARPANET), the predecessor of today's Internet, security was not a primary concern. Rather, leading computer scientists focused on developing network protocols with an openness that would allow many applications to be developed without constraint. [4] While this openness has generally resulted in many benefits, such as user-generated content, social networking, and e-commerce, cyberspace today is consequently plagued with a growing number of security vulnerabilities that can be, and often are, exploited by hackers, criminals, spies, terrorists, and even rogue nation states. Computer users in every domain are at risk for targeted computer attacks, identity theft, online fraud, spam, malware, denial of service, espionage, cyber terrorism, information warfare, and a growing number of other malicious cyber threats.

The ease of access, relative anonymity, and borderless nature of the Internet have allowed widespread computer-based crime – or cybercrime – to proliferate rapidly. Law enforcement and international security organizations, along with governments and the private sector, have only recently begun to appreciate the scope, severity and transnational nature of this problem. Additionally, with the dynamic growth and recent popularity of ICTs in developing countries around the world, these countries will likely experience a similarly steep learning curve in appreciating and combating this increasingly global proliferation of cyber threats.

In recent years, organizations have begun to emerge and evolve in a progressively collaborative ecosystem of vested international bodies seeking to address these challenges in unique, innovative ways. Such organizations today consist of international and regional telecommunication regulatory agencies, intergovernmental policymaking bodies, national homeland security agencies, regional law enforcement organizations, and various private-public and non-governmental organizations (NGOs) around the world. While many of these organizations are heavily focused on outreach, general education, and awareness-raising, some are also pursuing global collaboration, harmonization of statutory and regulatory provisions, and the development of incident readiness and response programs.[5]

This study attempts to address a series of questions regarding the current state of cyber security. What does the international landscape of cyber security look like today? What are these organizations actually doing? Are they succeeding? What measureable progress has been made in developing a supportive ecosystem of global cyber security? Are these organizations presenting practical, innovative, collaborative, and sustainable solutions to address these issues?

This study is the second phase of an initial attempt to survey and catalog the international, regional, private-public, and non-governmental organizations leading the global effort to secure cyberspace through local and regional policy initiatives, international harmonization of laws, basic research and technological innovation, law enforcement, education and training, incident response, and proliferation of secure ICTs.[6] This study focuses on categories of organizations which have to this date received little attention and exposure in the emerging international landscape of cyber security. Due to the sheer number of private organizations, national organizations, and infrastructure administration, maintenance, and operations organizations also active in the effort to secure cyberspace, the authors have chosen to omit discussion of these organizations at this time.

While the study currently catalogs approximately seventy organizations, it is by no means an exhaustive list. Only a dedicated research team can hope to maintain a comprehensive, up-to-date database of international cyber security organizations. Given the evolving nature of the Internet and global network infrastructures, as well as increasing public demand for information assurance and data privacy, the material in this study may very likely be out-of-date no sooner than the initial publication has been released. This study is also, by necessity, heavily reliant on information provided by the cataloged organizations' own websites, publications, articles, and meeting minutes from regional and international cybercrime conventions and public conferences. The authors invite readers to provide updates, corrections, omissions, and information on emerging organizations in order to continue and improve upon this repository.

To assist with forthcoming cataloging efforts, the authors of this book have collaborated to develop an initial web-based database of documented cyber security organizations. This catalog, which can be accessed online at http://www.cistp.gatech.edu/catalog/, is currently hosted by the Georgia Institute of Technology Center for International Strategy, Technology, and Policy (CISTP) and features a detailed description of each organization, including website links, relevant associations, and contact information. In addition, a full listing of abbreviations referenced throughout this book, as well as background and history of the current research initiative, can be accessed through the online catalog.

2 A Brief History of Global Responses to Cyber Threats

When the earliest implementations of packet switching networks were first developed by the United States government in the 1970s and early 1980s, certain researchers and computer scientists made substantial initial advances on securing these networks from cyber attacks and malicious exploits. However, as much of this research was conducted independently from the Advanced Research Projects Agency Network (ARPANET), many of these early ideas on network security and host authentication were neglected when ARPANET was transformed during the 1980s into what we call the Internet today. Following a 1983 study on the "possibility of an international application and harmonization of criminal laws to address the problem of computer crime and abuse," the Organisation for Economic Co-operation and Development (OECD, see Chapter 3) published *Computer-related Crime: Analysis of Legal Policy* in 1986.[7] The survey examined existing laws in member states, offered proposals for reforms, and recommended a "minimum list of abuses that countries should consider prohibiting and penalizing by criminal laws," attempting to serve as a common denominator between the different approaches taken by the member OECD countries.[8]

Following publication of the OECD report, the United Nations (UN, see Chapter 3) in 1990 adopted a resolution on computer crime legislation at its eighth Congress on the Prevention of Crime and Treatment of Offenders in Havana, Cuba.[9] This resolution was one of the first international efforts that addressed criminal laws related to computer crime. The resolution called upon member states to intensify their efforts to combat computer crime by modernizing national criminal laws, improving computer security and prevention measures, conducting adequate training, and collaborating on future efforts. Finally, the resolution called for the United Nations to promote international efforts in the development and dissemination of a comprehensive framework and standards that would assist the member states in dealing with computer-related crime.[10]

The first important international effort toward developing such a framework began in 1992 when the OECD issued *Guidelines for the Security of Information Systems and Networks*, intended for use by both the government and the private sector.[11] The framework document focused on nine principles: awareness, risk assessment, responsibility, response, security design and implementation, security management, reassessment, ethics, and democracy. The guidelines were reviewed in 1997 and 2001 by the OECD's Working Party on Information Security and Privacy (WPISP, see Chapter 3), and publication was accelerated in the aftermath of the September 11 attacks. The most recent guidelines were adopted in July 2002.[12]

In 2000, UN Resolution 55/63 was adopted by the General Assembly to combat the criminal misuse of information technology. Together with Resolution 56/121, passed in 2002, the UN called for the creation of measures to combat information technology misuse by stating: "...states should ensure that their laws and practices eliminate safe havens for those who criminally misuse information technologies..." and "...legal systems should protect the confidentiality, integrity, and availability of data and computer systems from unauthorized impairment and ensure the criminal abuse is penalized." [13] UN Resolutions 57/239 (2002) and 58/199 (2004) were later adopted to create "a global culture of cybersecurity and the protection of critical information infrastructures." [14]

2.1 World Summit on the Information Society (WSIS)

In 2001, the UN General Assembly called for the creation of a World Summit on the Information Society (WSIS, the Summit) in Resolution 56/183, where both public and private industries could "...harness synergies and create cooperation among the various information and communication technologies initiatives, at the regional and global levels." The International Telecommunication Union (ITU, see Chapter 3) was selected to serve in a managerial role over the Summit. The World Summit was held in two phases: in Geneva in December 2003 and Tunis in November 2005.[15] Reports from each summit were produced, with the latest update published in June 2007.[16]

The objective of the Geneva phase was to develop and foster a clear statement of political will and develop a plan for the foundations of an "...Information Society for all..." and a general plan of action ("Geneva Action Plan"). Following the meeting, two major areas were seen as important, "...building confidence, trust and security..." and "...establishing stable regulatory frameworks." [17] The WSIS Declaration of Principles, emphasizing a common vision and key principles for the Information Society, stated that "strengthening the trust framework, including information security and network security, authentication, privacy, and consumer protection, is a prerequisite for the development of the Information Society and for building confidence among users of ICTs." In order to achieve these objectives, a global culture of cyber security would need to be "actively promoted, developed, and implemented in cooperation with all stakeholders and international expert bodies." [18]

The ITU held a WSIS Thematic Meeting on Cybersecurity, hosted in Geneva from June 28 - July 1, 2005, to examine WSIS recommendations from the Geneva Summit (including the Action Plan and Declaration of Principles) related to building confidence and security in the use of ICTs and promotion of a global culture of cybersecurity. The meeting, open to all UN Member States, international organizations, WSIS accredited non-governmental organizations, ITU sector members, and civil society and accredited business entities, was structured to "consider and debate six broad themes in promoting international dialogue and cooperative measures among governments, the private sector, and other stakeholders, including:

- information sharing of national approaches, good practices and guidelines;
- developing watch, warning, and incident response capabilities;
- technical standards and industry solutions;
- harmonizing national legal approaches and international legal coordination;
- privacy, data and consumer protection;
- and developing countries and cybersecurity." [19]

At the Tunis Summit, WSIS reviewed and evaluated the progress on the Geneva Action Plan and devised the *Tunis Commitment* and the *Tunis Agenda for the Information Society*, which contained a comprehensive set of action items for involved parties. The identified action items initiated work to promote the spread of ICTs and clarify roles of public governance. Conference attendees planned to address a total of eleven broad action "lines." Action Line C5 ("Building confidence and security in the use of ICTs") reflects direct interest in cyber security and has been a focal point for many international and regional organizations, including the ITU and the Asia-Pacific Economic Cooperation (APEC, see Chapter 4).

Following the WSIS Tunis Summit in November 2005, the ITU presented a report on WSIS stocktaking and created a publicly accessible database of all WSIS-related implementation activities, including a number of projects related to cyber security and Action Line C5. The purpose of the WSIS Stocktaking Database was to be an "effective tool for the exchange of information on the projects fostering development of the information society, structured according to the eleven WSIS action lines." All WSIS stakeholders were encouraged to contribute information to the database, which would be continuously updated and maintained by the ITU.[20] The WSIS Stocktaking Database also complemented the ITU's *Golden Book: Stakeholder Commitments and Initiatives,* released in October 2005 to promote new commitments and initiatives announced by stakeholders at the Tunis Summit. The *Golden Book* database was frozen in January 2006, and a final report was published in February 2006.[21]

In addition to the WSIS Stocktaking Database and *Golden Book*, the ITU has since conducted annual facilitation meetings on WSIS Action Line C5 at its headquarters in Geneva. The first meeting, which took place in May 2006, was organized in line with WSIS paragraph 108 and the Annex of the Tunis Agenda for the Information Society, and was structured around the first five themes identified at the WSIS Thematic Meeting on Cybersecurity.[22] The second facilitation meeting, hosted in May 2007, was held in conjunction with several other events around the World Telecommunication and Information Society Day and focused on the issues of national strategies, legal frameworks, incident response, and spam and related threats.[23]

In May 2008, a third WSIS facilitation meeting- "Building Confidence and Security in the Use of ICTs"- was held at ITU headquarters in Geneva and focused on the legal, technical, and organizational challenges of cyber security, in addition to capacity building and international cooperation. The meeting's final report noted "a general view that ITU Global Cybersecurity Agenda was the appropriate framework for multi-stakeholder cooperation in cybersecurity and to concretize the role of ITU in this domain." In addition, proposals were made to ensure trust through technical solutions, establish frameworks in all domains, raise awareness, promote cooperation, and nominate "a centralized organization like the ITU with a structured framework" in the focus areas described above." [24]

In the 2007 *World Information Society Report: Beyond WSIS*, the ITU and the UN Conference on Trade and Development (UNCTAD) charted progress in building the Information Society and tracked the dynamics driving digital opportunity worldwide.[25] In chapter five, the report outlined primary challenges to building a safe and secure Information Society, including the recent evolution and increasing sophistication of threats such as spam, malware, and identity theft. The report identified primary mechanisms for taking action against these threats, as well as a roadmap for cyber security and the roles of different stakeholders, and encouraged themes such as information sharing, improvements in cyber security for developing economies, and promoted the ITU's Partnerships for Global Cybersecurity multi-stakeholder platform.[26]

2.2 Council of Europe Convention on Cybercrime

The Council of Europe's (COE, see Chapter 4) Convention on Cybercrime was the first international treaty of its kind seeking to address cybercrime by harmonizing national laws, improving investigative techniques, and increasing cooperation among nations. Created by the Council of Europe in 2001, the Convention represents the most prominent attempt at international harmonization of computer crime laws and procedures. According to the preamble, the main aim of the Convention is to pursue "…a common criminal policy aimed at the protection of society against cybercrime, *inter alia* by adopting appropriate legislation and fostering international co-operation." [27]

The Convention on Cybercrime took over four years and twenty-two substantive drafts before final approval by the Council of Europe in 2001. Significantly, it contains a series of powers and procedures, such as the search of computer networks and interception of network intruders. Containing forty-eight articles, the main focuses of the Convention are the normalization of definitions for computer-related offenses and the creation of a system for international cooperation. Additionally, the Convention includes definitions of investigation and prosecution procedures for use with global networks and multinational computer crimes. In particular, the convention includes a list of crimes that each signatory state must integrate into its own laws.

The criminalization of activities such as hacking, offenses related to child pornography, and specific intellectual property violations must be included.[28] The explanatory report associated with the Convention provides an interpretation that provides a basis for understanding. The following, based on the explanatory report, describe the contents of the Convention:

- Articles 2-13 address criminal law. Parties must domestically criminalize cybercrime, and offenses are divided into five categories. First, there are offenses against the confidentiality, integrity, and availability of computers, data, and systems (also known as CIA crimes). The second category involves the computer-related traditional offenses of forgery and fraud. Third are the content-related offenses of child pornography. The fourth category includes offenses related to copyright infringement and intellectual property. The final group consists of privacy infringement.
- Articles 14-22 address procedural law. Electronic evidence can be difficult to secure and can be quickly altered, moved, or deleted. The Convention requires each party to provide authorities with appropriate powers and procedures for use in investigations, including system search and seizure, real-time collection of traffic data, interception of content data, and the preservation and rapid disclosure of computer-stored data relating to traffic.
- Articles 23-35 address international cooperation. The Convention's provisions for international cooperation are subject to the domestic laws of the parties, as well as existing international agreements, such as MLATs (Mutual Legal Agreement Treaty). The Convention seeks to provide mechanisms for mutual assistance, in the event that existing international agreements are not applicable, or to expedite existing agreements. The 24/7 Network, intended to handle requests for mutual assistance quickly and efficiently (Art. 35), attempts to expedite international cooperation. Each party is required to designate a point of contact to facilitate rapid investigation of cybercrimes, similar to the Group of Eight's (G8, see Chapter 3) High-Tech Crime 24/7 Point-of-Contact Network. The 24/7 networks are expected to communicate rapidly with their peers in other locations, and the parties must ensure that trained and equipped personnel are available to staff the network.
- Articles 36-42 are largely administrative and address declarations and reservations with the treaty, for which the drafters have allowed considerable flexibility in interpretation in order to ensure wide acceptance. Through "declarations," parties may propose additional elements in their interpretations of offenses and procedural obligations, and through "reservations" parties may limit or qualify those same obligations. [29]

In November 2002, the Council of Europe introduced an *Additional Protocol to the Convention on Cybercrime*, which addressed the criminalization of racist and xenophobic acts committed through computer systems and entailed an extension of the Convention's scope, including its substantive, procedural, and international cooperation provisions.

Since its introduction in 2001, the Convention on Cybercrime has been ratified by twenty-three countries and signed, but not yet ratified, by another twenty-two (see Appendix B for a complete listing of all current Convention on Cybercrime signatories). As of August 2008, all but six of the forty-seven Council of Europe members have signed the Convention, and over ten nations, including the United States, have ratified the Convention in the last three years.[30] An analysis of the impact of the Convention on Cybercrime, as well as a brief discussion on early debates regarding its approach to privacy and data retention, are further examined in Chapter 3.

3 International Intergovernmental Organizations

Cyber security is attracting focused attention from international governing, policymaking, law enforcement, and security bodies, including the United Nations (UN), the Organisation for Economic Co-operation and Development (OECD), the North Atlantic Treaty Organization (NATO), and INTERPOL. In particular, the growing issue of cybercrime has become a primary focus for many of these organizations' subordinate sectors and working groups, such as the International Telecommunication Union (ITU) – an autonomous, specialized agency of the UN – and the OECD Working Party on Information Security and Privacy (WPISP). This section catalogs several international organizations committed to promoting cyber security and building confidence and security in the use of ICTs.

3.1 United Nations (UN)

The United Nations, established in 1945 by fifty-one countries "committed to preserving peace through international cooperation and collective security," is an international network of 192 countries working to "maintain international peace and security, to develop friendly relations among nations, to cooperate in solving international problems and in promoting respect for human rights, and to be a centre in harmonizing the actions of nations." [31] With respect to cyber security, the UN has pledged support for ICT capacity-building and global anti-terrorism initiatives. The International Telecommunication Union, discussed in greater detail below, is the UN-affiliated organization most responsible for directing these efforts.

3.1.1 International Telecommunication Union (ITU)

The ITU, originally named the International Telegraph Union, was founded by network operators to allow interconnection and interoperability of national facilities and services.[32] Today the ITU's main tasks include standardization, allocation of the radio spectrum, and organization of interconnection arrangements between different countries to allow international phone calls. As of April 2008, the ITU's membership includes 191 member states and over 700 private companies and other organizations. It is also the only intergovernmental organization within the UN system that has partnerships between government and industry.[33]

With regard to cyber security, the fundamental roles of the ITU, following WSIS and the 2006 ITU Plenipotentiary Conference, are to build confidence and security in the use of ICTs, facilitate cooperation among public and private organizations, and foster education and training initiatives. Global leaders participating in WSIS and ITU Member States entrust the ITU to take concrete steps towards curbing the threats and vulnerabilities related to the information society. [34]

In facilitation of Action Line C5 of WSIS, the ITU has encouraged ongoing cooperation among its three core sectors- the ITU Telecommunication Standardization Sector (ITU-T), the ITU Telecommunication Development Sector (ITU-D), and the ITU Radiocommunication Sector (ITU-R)- together with the ITU Corporate Strategy Division (CSD) and the ITU Strategy & Policy Unit (SPU), to address key issues related to cyber security in conjunction with an open, multi-stakeholder platform ("Partnerships for Global Cybersecurity (PGC)"). The ITU's two most significant achievements in this area have been the Global Cybersecurity Agenda (described in greater detail below) and the Cybersecurity Gateway- an online information resource on national and international cyber initiatives worldwide, through which users can obtain information regarding different initiatives on a country-by-country basis in several different areas, including: information sharing, watch and warning, industry standards and solutions, laws and legislation, and privacy and protection. [35]

In Plenipotentiary Resolution 130 (Antalya 2006), the ITU was requested to give high priority to building confidence and security in the use of information and communication technologies, [36] and in Resolution 149 (Antalya 2006) to clarify definitions and terminology relating to building confidence and security in the use of ICTs. [37] In order to raise awareness, the ITU has since organized a series of regional workshops on Frameworks for Cybersecurity and Critical Information Infrastructure Protection. Jointly organized by ITU-D and ITU-T, the purpose of these workshops has been to achieve the following objectives:

- Identify challenges faced by countries in the Americas in developing frameworks for cyber security and CIIP, share experiences, and consider best practices;
- Disseminate information on the *ITU Cybersecurity Work Programme to Assist Developing Countries* and ITU-D Study Group Question 22/1: *Securing information and communication networks: Best practices for developing a culture of cyber security;*
- Disseminate information on related technical security standards activities developed/being developed by standardization organizations, and in particular, related ITU-T activities;
- and Review the role of various actors (e.g., governments, service providers, academia, citizens, etc.) in promoting a culture of cyber security. [38]

The first regional workshop, hosted in Hanoi, Vietnam in August 2007, responded to requests by international telecommunication assemblies to "undertake initiatives to bridge the standardization gap between developed and developing countries and strengthen the collaboration between ITU-D and ITU-T respectively." This workshop, targeting policy makers, regulators, service providers, and operators, responded by providing a review of ITU-T cyber security-related recommendations and activities and informing participants on related ITU-D Study Group activities. [39] The next regional workshop was held in Buenos Aires, Argentina in October 2007 and had a structure and purpose similar to that of its predecessor. [40] Subsequent workshops, including the West Africa Workshop on Policy and Regulatory Frameworks and CIIP, held in Praia, Cape Verde in November 2007 [41] and the Regional Workshop on Frameworks for Cybersecurity and CIIP & Cybersecurity Forensics Workshop, held in Doha, Qatar in February 2008 continued to pursue these goals with a greater focus on regional infrastructures and further attention to recent issues, such as cyber security forensics. [42]

All three ITU core sectors, as well as the ITU Corporate Strategy Division and Strategy & Policy Unit, have spent a considerable amount of time and effort the past several years developing and promoting ongoing cyber security initiatives in the global effort to promote a global culture of cyber security. The following efforts highlight only a sample of current initiatives and accomplishments on which the various ITU sectors have remained active and diligent.

3.1.1.1 ITU Telecommunication Standardization Sector (ITU-T)

On October 4, 2004, ITU-T hosted a Cybersecurity Symposium in Florianópolis, Brazil, in order to address global concern for cyber security by providing an organized forum for discussion on practical experiences highlighting major security threats to ICTs. The primary goal of the symposium was to "bring together senior managers from administrations, computer emergency response teams (CERTs), network operators, and equipment manufacturers to discuss the current state of cybersecurity, and consider future approaches to ensure security in cyberspace." [43] In March, 2005, ITU-T hosted a second Cybersecurity Symposium in Moscow, Russian Federation, in order to highlight the significance of cyber security standardization as an integral component of ICTs.[44]

The World Telecommunication Standardization Assembly (WTSA), which supports the implementation of general policy mechanisms and working methods for ITU-T, convened following the first symposium "with a plan for future global standards-setting and a clear statement about the direction of the future work of ITU-T." With 475 delegates representing seventy-five countries, WTSA-04 deliberated on several key issues pertinent to cyber security, such as next generation networks (NGN), bridging the standardization gap between developing and developed countries, consensual decision-making, new resolutions on Internet-related issues, and the adoption of a resolution on cyber security (*WTSA Resolution 50*) including the following key initiatives: [45]

- ITU-T should evaluate new, existing, and evolving recommendations, and especially signaling and communications protocol recommendations, with respect to their robustness of design and potential for exploitation by malicious parties to interfere destructively with their deployment in the global ICT infrastructure;
- ITU-T should continue to raise awareness, within its area of operation and influence, of the need to defend information and communication systems against the threat of cyber attack and continue to promote cooperation among appropriate entities in order to enhance the exchange of technical information in the field ICT network security. [46]

WTSA-04 also adopted separate resolutions to address issues specifically related to spam. In particular, *WTSA Resolution 51: Combating Spam* was adopted to emphasize the urgency in identifying relevant initiatives by the ITU and other international organizations for addressing the problem and to encourage Member States "to take appropriate steps within their national legal frameworks to ensure that appropriate and effective measures are taken to combat spam." [47] In *WTSA Resolution 52: Countering spam by technical means*, WTSA requested relevant ITU-T study groups to cooperate with the Internet Engineering Task Force (IETF) and other pertinent organizations to prepare for the Telecommunication Standardization Advisory Group a set of technical recommendations for countering spam. [48] WTSA is planning its next conference (WTSA-08) in October 2008 in Johannesburg, South Africa, immediately following a Global Standards Symposium. Although planning for the summit is still in its early stages, WTSA-08 will be expected to again define general policy and adopt working methods and procedures for ITU-T. [49]

In addition to WTSA, ITU-T has also hosted numerous other workshops and conferences to effect cyber security standards in the information society. The ITU held a Workshop on "New Horizons for Security Standardization" in Geneva in October 2005, a meeting in 2006 to discuss standards for single sign-on, the annual Broadband Europe conference, and the Workshop on Digital Identity for NGN in December 2006. [50]

ITU-T Study Group 17, the lead telecommunication security group, has been especially active in promoting cyber security initiatives, providing numerous forums and focus groups in which topics on security guidance, identity management, and security standards may be presented. [51] In addition, Study Group 17 recently collaborated with the European Network and Information Security Agency (ENISA, see Chapter 4) and the Network and Information Security Steering Group (NISSG, see Chapter 5) to produce the ICT Security Standards Roadmap. The roadmap, released as an updated version in December 2007, was developed to "aid the process of [security] standards development [and] provide information that will help potential users of security standards, and other standards stakeholders, gain an understanding of what standards are available or under development as well as the key organizations that are working on these standards." In May 2007, Part 5 of the roadmap ("Best Practices") was converted into a searchable database format. [52]

3.1.1.2 ITU Telecommunication Development Sector (ITU-D)

"The ICT Applications and Cybersecurity Division (CYB) is the ITU Tele-communication Development Sector's (ITU-D) focal point to assist developing countries through the use of information and communication technologies (ICTs) and telecommunication networks, to advance the achievement of national, regional and the internationally agreed development goals, by promoting the use of ICT-based products, networks, services and applications, and to help countries overcome the digital divide." [53]

CYB's main contribution is the coordination of ITU efforts in the expansion of telecommunications in developing countries. The *Cybersecurity Guide for Developing Countries* is an annual guide designed to increase the understanding of developing countries regarding some of the issues relating to ICT security and to provide them with examples of solutions that other nations have implemented in order to deal with these problems. It also references additional publications with more specific information on cyber security. As stated in the 2007 version of the document, "the content of the guide has been selected to meet the needs of developing and, in particular, least developed countries, in terms of the use of information and communication technologies for the provision of basic services in different sectors, while remaining committed to developing local potential and increasing awareness among all of the stakeholders." [54] CYB also drafted the *ITU Cybersecurity Work Programme to Assist Developing Countr*ies in December 2007[55] and offers its ICT Eye Website to aid developing nations in collecting data for reports and security policies.[56]

CYB is also working on a Botnet Mitigation Toolkit, which will "seek to raise awareness among Member States of the growing threats posed by botnets and the linkage with criminal activities, and [will] incorporate policy, technical, and social aspects of mitigating the effects of botnets." The toolkit, which will be pilot tested in a number of member states in 2008, will draw on existing resources, identify relevant stakeholders, and take into consideration the constraints posed by developing economies. [57]

Based on studies from the ITU-D Study Group 1, Question 22/1: *Securing information and communication networks: best practices for developing a culture of cybersecurity*, the ITU has developed a National Cybersecurity/CIIP Self-

Assessment Toolkit for national leadership at the policy and management levels of government in member states. This toolkit is intended to "assist national governments in examining their existing national policies, procedures, norms, institutions, and relationships in light of national need to enhance cybersecurity and address critical information infrastructure protection." The draft toolkit, including an Annex on Deterring Cybercrime: Substantive, Procedural, and Mutual Assistance Law Baseline Survey, was made publicly available in January 2008. [58]

In collaboration with an international group of experts, including the American Bar Association (ABA, see Chapter 5), the ITU will also be releasing a draft version of the ITU Toolkit for Cybercrime Legislation in early 2008. This toolkit, focusing on the national cyber security/CIIP strategy element of deterring cybercrime, aims to "provide countries with reference material that can assist in the establishment of a legislative framework to deter cybercrime" and can be used in conjunction with the National Cybersecurity/CIIP Self-Assessment Toolkit Annex on Deterring Cybercrime. [59]

ITU-D recently announced the Regional Cybersecurity Forum for Europe and CIS planned for October 2008 in Sofia, Bulgaria which will focus on identifying regional challenges in developing frameworks for cyber security, consider best practices, share information on ITU development activities, and review the role of other actors in promoting a global culture of cyber security. In addition, the ITU will develop for the forum a Report on Best Practices for a National Approach to Cybersecurity which outlines a Framework for Organizing a National Approach to Cybersecurity by identifying the following key elements of a national effort:

1. Developing a national cyber security strategy;
2. Establishing national government-industry collaboration;
3. Creating a national incident management capability;
4. Deterring cybercrime; and
5. Promoting a national culture of cyber security. [60]

ITU-D has also been active planning other regional workshops and events, such as the World Telecommunication Development Conference (WTDC-06) in Doha, Qatar, in March 2006 and the Regional Workshop on e-Signatures and Identity Management in Damascus, Syria, in October 2007. In particular, WTDC-06 attracted nearly a thousand participants representing 132 countries. The Doha Declaration stressed the need to quicken the "pace towards the creation of a truly global Information Society in order to bring opportunities to countries, and to create conditions aimed at deriving maximum benefit from the implementation of new services and applications in order to accelerate overall development." [61] A roadmap was declared in the Doha Action Plan to implement ICT development objectives in the next four years at the national, regional, and international levels.[62] In particular, Programme 3 ("e-Strategies and ICT applications") described specific priorities related to cyber security, including security in Internet Protocols, ICT applications, and telecommunication devices, as well as e-strategies and Internet multilingualization.[63]

3.1.1.3 ITU Radiocommunication Sector (ITU-R)

The primary contribution of ITU-R to the global cyber security initiative is including references to security in its numerous ITU-R recommendations. Series 'S' Recommendations, which contain references to security, include S.1250: *Network management architecture for digital satellite systems forming part of SDH transport networks in the fixed satellite service* and S.1711: *Performance enhancements of transmission control protocol over satellite networks.* Recommendations particularly relevant to cyber security include Recommendation 1078: *Security principles for IMT-2000* and Recommendation 1223: *Evaluation of security mechanisms for IMT-2000.* Security mechanisms in IMT-2000 are also referenced in Recommendation 1457, and references to security in other systems can be found in Recommendations M.1645 and M.2063. [64]

3.1.1.4 ITU Corporate Strategy Division (CSD)

The ITU Corporate Strategy Division (CSD) assists the ITU and its sectors by analyzing the challenges facing the telecommunication and ICT environment and identifying their strategic implications for stakeholders, including member states and the industry. With particular relevance to cyber security, CSD works to identify trends in the evolution of cyber security, spam, and cybercrime, and establishes corporate strategy objectives for the ITU. [65] CSD also maintains an updated page on its website regarding cyber security-related activities of the ITU Corporate Strategy, called the Cybersecurity Watch News log.[66]

The Global Cybersecurity Agenda (GCA) was created by CSD to tackle cybercrime within a framework of international cooperation. The goal of the GCA is "to foster a common understanding of the importance of cyber security and bring together all relevant stakeholders (governments, intergovernmental organizations, the private sector, and civil society) to work on concrete solutions to deal with cybercrime." The Global Cybersecurity Agenda has a two-year timetable and rests on five pillars:

1. Finding technical solutions for every environment
2. Developing interoperable legislative frameworks
3. Building capacity in all relevant areas
4. Establishing appropriate organizational structures
5. Adopting effective international cooperation mechanisms [67]

In a historic visit to the ITU in July 2007, UN Secretary-General Ban Ki-Moon expressed satisfaction with the focus of the ITU Global Cybersecurity Agenda on least developed countries. In addition, the President of the Republic of Costa Rica and Nobel Peace Laureate Dr. Óscar Arias Sánchez, in a foreword to the ITU Global Cybersecurity Agenda, praised the GCA for its ability to "match hackers' international range, and allow rapid coordination between countries at the national and global levels." [68]

In facilitation of CSD's objectives on cyber security, the office of the ITU Secretary General organized the High-Level Experts Group on Cybersecurity (HLEG), including experts from governments, industry, regional/international organizations, research institutes, and academic institutions, with the following responsibilities to the Secretary General:

- To further develop the Global Cybersecurity Agenda, by proposing refinements to its main goals.
- To analyze current developments in cybersecurity, including both threats and state-of-the-art solutions, anticipate emerging and future challenges, identify strategic options, and formulate proposals to the ITU Secretary-General.
- To meet the goals of the Global Cybersecurity Agenda.
- To provide guidance on possible long-term strategies and emerging trends in cybersecurity.

In 2007, CSD commissioned A Generic National Framework for Critical Information Infrastructure Protection (CIIP), in conjunction with the ITU-D Cybersecurity Division, in order to "outline a simple framework that could be of interest to developing countries interested in establishing a national program for critical information infrastructure protection." By promoting the "Four-Pillar Model" of CIIP, the document focuses on prevention and early warning, detection, reaction, and crisis management for functional CIIP units. [69]

3.1.1.5 WSIS Thematic Meeting on Countering Spam

The ITU has been extremely active in promoting anti-spam initiatives. In particular, the ITU hosted the WSIS Thematic Meeting on Countering Spam in July 2004 in Geneva, Switzerland, in preparation for the WSIS Tunis Summit in November 2005. In response to the *WSIS Declaration of Principles and Action Plan* adopted in 2003, it was recognized that spam was a "significant and growing problem for users, networks, and the Internet as a whole," and that it would be necessary to take "appropriate action on spam at the national and international levels." [70] With approximately two hundred participants, including government policymakers and regulators, international and intergovernmental organizations, ICT companies, academics, industry professionals, and others, the event focused on identifying the scope of the problem, as well as technical solutions, promoting consumer education and awareness, discussing spam legislation and enforcement, the need for multilateral and bilateral cooperation, and agreeing on frameworks for international action.[71]

In the Chairman's final report, it was noted that because there is no "silver bullet" to resolving the problem of spam, only a "multi-pronged approach to solving the problem, involving all stakeholders, [is] clearly necessary. The combination of technical solutions, user awareness, appropriate and balanced legislation followed up with measured enforcement, industry initiatives including those by the marketing community, and international cooperation, are seen as key elements." [72] In addition to spam, phishing and fraudulent online activity were also seen as major threats to public confidence in ICTs.

Following the WSIS Thematic Meeting on Countering Spam, the ITU launched a comprehensive online database devoted to all spam-related issues, including background resources, documentation, presentations, contributions, and technical papers on the issues presented at the event, including spam legislation and enforcement, technical solutions, international cooperation, and consumer education and awareness. Additionally, the ITU provides detailed information on upcoming spam-related conferences and events hosted by partners in the international community, such as StopSpamAlliance.org. [73] The ITU also revisited the topic of countering spam on the first day of the 2005 WSIS Thematic Meeting on Cybersecurity in Geneva, Switzerland. [74]

In April 2008, ITU-T Study Group 3 published a report on the *Financial Aspects of Network Security: Malware and Spam* in an effort to identify recent malware and spam developments, present a framework for analyzing related financial flows, document primary empirical research findings, offer a preliminary welfare assessment, and recognize the underground malware/spam economy of spammers, botnet herders, and malware writers and distributors. Several key recommendations were also submitted by the Study Group to the ITU Standardization Sector for approval, including technical strategies, technologies involved, and a technical framework for countering email spam.[75]

3.1.1.6 World Trust Signatories Association (WTSA)

The World e-Trust Initiative, established by ITU-D in 2002 to facilitate a highly secure ICT infrastructure for developing countries, attracted significant attention for its efforts to promote authentic, secure online communications by combining "centuries-old certification processes, proven public key infrastructure, and methods borrowed from the world of physical architecture and construction." The World e-Trust Memorandum of Understanding was made available for signing by ITU member nations and sector member organizations in an effort to resolve problems of authenticity by re-examining assumptions upon which the Internet was founded. [76]

Since the World e-Trust Initiative was launched in 2002, governments, the private sector, and civil society representing thirty-five countries have signed the World e-Trust Memorandum of Understanding.[77] The World Trust Signatories Association (WTSA) was founded for all organizations who have signed the World e-Trust Memorandum of Understanding and for individuals who have signed the WTSA Memorandum of Support. "Committed to bringing the benefits of reliable certification to the online world," WTSA ensures that all certification in the World e-Trust Initiative is conducted by duly constituted public authority.[78] Partnering with Quiet Enjoyment Infrastructure (QEI), in March 2005 the ITU introduced the City of Osmio, an online-only municipality, as an experiment to demonstrate authenticity over the World Wide Web using trusted public key infrastructure and digital certificates.[79]

3.1.2 United Nations Office on Drugs and Crime (UNODC)

UNODC, a United Nations agency originally founded in 1997 as the Office for Drug Control and Crime Prevention, was established to help the UN address the interrelated issues of illicit-drug control, crime prevention, and international terrorism. This intent is fulfilled through three primary functions: research, lobbying state governments to adopt various crime and drug based laws and treaties, and assistance of said governments on the ground level. [80]

UNODC, focusing specifically on the criminal misuse and falsification of identity, has been particularly interested in helping with the implementation of WSIS Action Line C5 ("building confidence and security in the use of ICTs") for its specific reference to cybercrime. UNODC initiatives include the promotion of cybercrime legislation, law enforcement, and training programs. At the 2nd Facilitation Meeting for WSIS Action Line C5 in May 2007, UNODC presented the results of "a study on fraud and the criminal misuse and falsification of identity," drafted initially for the Commission on Crime Prevention and Criminal Justice in Vienna in April 2007.[81] In its report, UNODC recommended that Member States "develop and implement effective fraud- [and identity-related crime] prevention measures at the national, regional, and global levels, and in cooperation with the private sector." In addition, the agency recommended training, collaboration, and the sharing of technical information among member states and with developing countries and other intergovernmental bodies. [82]

In January 2007, UNODC hosted the Cyber Crime Training Programme in Kerala, India, in association with Microsoft and the Kerala Police, focusing on "online crimes against children in the context of growing criminal use of the Internet for child abuse and human trafficking" and "address[ed] the need for enhancing the technical capacity of the law enforcement agencies in dealing with [cyber] criminal activities." The first such programme, Advanced Forensic Training on Cyber Crime and Computer-facilitated Crimes against Children, was organized in Ghaziabad, India, in October 2006. [83] UNODC has also referenced cybercrime legislation and prevention in the 2004 Report on the Expert Group Meeting on Technical Assistance Guidelines[84] and in the 2006 Policing: Crime Investigation "Criminal justice assessment toolkit," [85] as well as at numerous regional workshops, seminars, and conferences around the world.

UNODC also organized the Global Financial Crime Congress, together with INTERPOL, from April 17-20, 2007, in Bangkok, Thailand, to discuss new developments, technologies, and strategies used to counter financial crime [including cybercrime], and to encourage cooperation between law enforcement agencies and the private sector. "At the Congress, experts from law enforcement, customs, academia, private industry, and multilateral organizations learned about training initiatives by UNODC targeting different areas of financial crime." [86]

3.1.3 United Nations Office for Disarmament Affairs (UNODA)

The United Nations Office for Disarmament Affairs (UNODA), established in 1982 and later reformed in 1998, works to "promote the goal of nuclear disarmament and non-proliferation and the strengthening of the disarmament regimes in respect to other weapons of mass destruction, chemical and biological weapons." In addition, UNODA "fosters preventive disarmament measures, such as dialogue, transparency and confidence building on military matters, and encourages regional disarmament efforts." [87]

In recent years, UNODA has expanded its focus on cyber terrorism and information warfare. In August 2001, UNODA presented a report on the "Revolution in Information Technology and its impact on Security" to the United Nations Conference on Disarmament Issues at "The Asian Pacific Region: Evolution of the Scope of Security and Disarmament in the 21st Century" in Ishikawa – Kanazawa, Japan. In the plenary report, UNODA acknowledged a growing threat of sophisticated cyber attacks, information warfare, and electronic espionage in an increasingly technological world, and encouraged public diplomacy, cyber arms control, and the promotion of public awareness to fill the "knowledge gap." [88]

3.2 Organisation for Economic Co-operation and Development (OECD)

The Organisation for Economic Co-operation and Development is an international forum bringing together the governments of thirty member countries, as of 2008, committed to democracy and market economies. The organization provides a setting where governments compare policy experiences, seek answers to common problems, identify good practices, and coordinate domestic and international policies. The associated Working Party on Information Security and Privacy (WPISP) is primarily devoted to education and data gathering and publishes "Guidelines for the Security of Information Systems and Networks." [89] Furthermore, the Working Party annually surveys member nations on implementation of these guidelines and publishes the guide, *Privacy Online: OECD Guidance on Policy and Practice*, which attempts to gauge current trends and issues in cyberspace.

Another report, *Policies for the Protection of Critical Information Infrastructure*, offers an "analysis of the Critical Information Infrastructure (CII) security policies in four OECD member countries that volunteered for the study. It examines how risks to the CII are assessed and managed in general terms, what the emerging and existing models are for public-private information sharing, and the national responses to the growing need for cross border collaboration. The report identifies similarities and differences in policies for protecting the CII across the volunteer countries. It helps readers understand how governments coordinate with owners and operators of CII systems and networks beyond their authority, within and across borders, and how they keep their policies and programs for protecting the CII updated. It includes best practices for the development of policies in this area and seeks to promote the sharing of knowledge and experience between the volunteer countries, other OECD countries, and non-members. The report's ultimate goal is to foster a better understanding of how to protect the CII and to increase international cooperation." [90]

A third report, the *Promotion of a Culture of Security for Information Systems and Networks*, includes a detailed inventory of effective national initiatives to implement the 2002 OECD *Guidelines for the Security of Information Systems and Networks: Towards a Culture of Security*. Prepared by the OECD Secretariat based on responses from eighteen OECD member countries to a questionnaire circulated in November 2004, the analysis, synthesis, and summary of responses contained in the report were current as of September 2005 and were all to be read as an *interpretation* of the information provided. [91]

The 2005 OECD report followed a previous report released in 2003, which offered a summary of responses to the survey on the implementation of the OECD Guidelines.[92] At its eighteenth meeting in May 2005 in Paris, France, WPISP discussed a first draft of the new report and agreed to finalize it by written procedure. The Committee for Information, Computer, and Communications Policy (ICCP) discussed the report at its forty-ninth meeting in October 2005 and declassified it by written procedure in November 2005. The main findings from this report were as follows:

1. "e-Government and the protection of national critical infrastructures appear[ed] to be two main drivers for developing a culture of security at the national level."
2. "International co-operation [was] consolidated in the area of cybercrime and Computer Emergency Response Teams (CERTs)."
3. "Member countries [were] adopting a multidisciplinary and multistakeholder approach and establishing a high-level governance structure for the implementation of national policies," including the development of a national policy framework and legal frameworks for combating cybercrime, as well as information sharing and awareness raising.
4. Finally, the report showed that "responding countries seem[ed] to have devoted less attention to developing research and development for information security, metrics and benchmarks for measuring the effectiveness of their national policies, and initiatives for co-ordinated frameworks to address the specific needs of small- and medium-sized enterprises (SMEs)." [93]

In a report from the 2003 OECD Oslo Global Forum on Information Systems and Networks Security: Towards a Culture of Security, it was suggested that government and business leadership, together with strong public-private partnerships, would be critical to implementing the OECD Security Guidelines. In addition, the impact of measures for information security should be reviewed, and better methodologies, benchmarks, and metrics should be developed. Further information sharing and exchange of best practices is necessary, improved education and training should be encouraged in non-member nations, and interdependencies should be promoted between developed and developing countries. [94]

The joint OECD-APEC Workshop on Security of Information Systems and Networks was held in Seoul, South Korea, September 5-6, 2005, in conjunction with the 32nd APEC TEL meeting (APEC, see Chapter 4). The focus of the workshop was to exchange policy and strategies for developing a culture of security, share experiences on effective initiatives, and identify and prioritize future cooperation between the two groups on addressing security-related issues. In particular, the report recognized the need for further cooperation on research and analysis of evolving threats (such as malware), wireless and mobile security, and information sharing and response. [95]

WPISP recently launched a dedicated Culture of Security Website to assist OECD member and non-member countries to share policies and best practices to help promote a culture of security. According to the website, "security must become an integral part of the daily routine of individuals, businesses, and governments in their use of ICTs and conduct of online activities." The site contains links to recent events, presentations, initiatives, conferences, toolkits, guidelines, regional workshops, and news articles, all related to cyber security and the OECD Security Guidelines. [96]

In addition to general policy and information security awareness initiatives, WPISP has also been involved in numerous research and analysis activities related to cyber security threats, including the development of OECD Guidelines on Cryptography Policy (1998), the OECD Task Force on Spam (2005-2006), the Indicators for Trust initiative (2005), a report on Biometric-based Technologies (2004), as well as initiatives with e-Authentication, digital identity management, malware, and a common framework for implementing information security and privacy. [97]

In particular, WPISP recently organized the APEC-OECD Workshop on Malware in April 2007 in Manila, Philippines, to identify the evolving landscape of malware, as well as challenges in properly addressing it and available mechanisms to combat its spread and mitigate its effects. In the summary report, members agreed to focus on operational, cross-border cooperation against malware and cyber attacks and strategic collaboration among stakeholders. [98] At the OECD Workshop on Digital Identity Management (IDM) in Trondheim, Norway, in May 2007, experts from government, industry, and civil society were brought together to discuss information security and privacy issues related to digital identity management. The primary focus of the workshop was to discuss the "broader implications of IDM for individuals' ability to control the digital representation of their identity and its potential uses." [99] Members agreed to take further action on defining what constitutes digital identity and articulating the benefits of identity management systems for different stakeholders.[100]

In June 2007, WPISP, in collaboration with APEC TEL (see Chapter 4), presented a report entitled "Malicious Software (Malware): A Security Threat to the Internet Economy" at the OECD Ministerial Meeting on the Future of the Internet Economy in Seoul, Korea. Main points from the Ministerial Background Report included recommended strategies for global partnerships against malware "to avoid it from becoming a serious threat to the Internet economy and to national security in the coming years" and aimed to "inform policy makers about malware impacts, growth and evolution, and countermeasures to combat malware." In working to promote its goals, the report suggested organizing a global "Anti-Malware Partnership" including governments, the private sector, the technical community, and civil society "to produce joined-up policy guidance to fight malware on all fronts from educational to technical to legal to economical." [101]

3.3 North Atlantic Treaty Organization (NATO)

The North Atlantic Treaty Organization (NATO) is an alliance of twenty-six countries from North America and Europe that provides an international forum for the discussion of common security issues.[102] In 1969, NATO established the Committee on the Challenges of Modern Society (CCMS), which argued for "the introduction of a non-military focus within the alliance..." to address "...increasing societal vulnerabilities from sources beyond the traditional security framework." [103] Since the 1970s, NATO has played an extensive role in developing internetwork computer communications with the U.S. Defense Advanced Research Projects Agency (DARPA), including improvements in cyber security capabilities, infrastructure, and technology throughout the 1990s.[104] However, as the international threat of cyber terrorism and information warfare became a greater reality following the September 11, 2001, attacks, NATO presented a report entitled "Vulnerability of the Interconnected Society" in Oslo, Norway, in October 2002. Specifically, the report asserted increasing attention to cyber security vulnerabilities and the growing need for improvements in crisis management, communication, cyber security, capacity building, multidisciplinary information sharing, and interdependencies among critical infrastructures.[105]

Following the 2002 Prague Summit in Czech Republic, NATO leaders directed the establishment of the NATO Cyber Defense Programme, including the three-phased creation of the currently functioning NATO Computer Incident Response Capability - Technical Centre (NCIRC TC). At the 2006 Riga Summit in Latvia, NATO further acknowledged the need for longer-term protection of information systems and prepared an assessment report on its approach to cyber defense to Allied Defense Ministers in October 2007.[106]

NATO defense ministers recently agreed to intensify their studies regarding the prevention of cyber attacks even more aggressively following an onslaught on Estonia's public cyberspace in 2007 "...controlling banking, email, and other functions..." In this attack, criminals located in over fifty countries crippled Estonia's most crucial day-to-day activities. This demonstrated to the organization the necessity for the implementation of Internet security on a wider basis, and that the issue was clearly a global one based on the international nature of the crime. [107]

Consequently, NATO established the Cyber Defense Center of Excellence in Estonia in 2008. Seven member countries who expressed a wish to participate met in January 2008 to finalize and approve the language of an agreement,[108] the Cyber Defense Concept,[109] expected to be endorsed by heads of state and government at the Bucharest Summit in Romania in April 2008.[110] The initiative will include creation of a Cyber Defense Management Authority, bringing together key actors in NATO's cyber defense activities to "manage cyber defense across all NATO's communication and information systems and support individual Allies in defending against cyber attacks upon request." [111]

NATO also maintains a catalog of information security and information assurance products in a web-based database, publicly available in its unclassified form. According to its website, the catalog "...brings together all InfoSec and IA products into one all-encompassing dynamic web-based catalogue, which will enable the NATO community an easier process for finding InfoSec and IA products that are evaluated and suitable for use in the NATO environment." [112]

The Science for Peace and Security (SPS) Committee is the primary NATO committee supporting practical cooperation in civil science and innovation, including initiatives related to network security and cyber terrorism. The group conducted an Advanced Research Workshop (ARW) on "Cyber Terrorism as a New Security Threat" in Sofia, Bulgaria, in 2006, at which experts from member, partner, and non-member nations gathered to discuss the need to research areas such as the interaction between cyber terrorism and organized crime, the role of governments and international organizations on fighting and preventing cyber-crime, and security measures, such as biometrics, cryptography, wireless network security, and computer forensics. Workshop members concurred that "theoretically feasible acts of cyber terrorism should not be overlooked." [113]

3.4 Group of Eight (G8)

The Group of Eight (G8) is an international forum for the governments of Canada, France, Germany, Italy, Japan, Russia, the United Kingdom, and the United States. As of 2005, these countries collectively represent approximately 65% of the global economy, as measured by gross domestic product.[114] The G8 Subgroup on High Tech Crime is an attempt to provide information sharing mechanisms among the major industrialized powers. Specifically, the Subgroup's mission is to "...enhance the abilities of G8 countries to prevent, investigate, and prosecute crimes involving computers, networked communications, and other new technologies." [115]

Scott Charney, chairman of the G8 Subgroup on High Tech Crime, in June 1999, further clarified that the intended objectives of the Subgroup were to guarantee the criminalization of cybercrime both inside and outside the jurisdiction of G8 member countries, to create guidelines for other countries, to accelerate procedures for transnational tasks, to ensure an increasingly coordinated response to cyber attacks, to guarantee that juridical systems are arranged for maximum efficiency, and to identify the interaction between the needs for prosecution and those of the market. In the context of Subgroup initiatives, Charney was also tasked with addressing issues such as international harmonization efforts, cryptography, standardization of new technologies for prosecution purposes, and surveillance capabilities of Internet Service Providers (ISPs). [116]

The group's most significant contribution has been the creation and promotion of its 24/7 Network of Contacts for High-Tech Crime, described in more detail in the Incident Response section below. The G8 Subgroup on High Tech Crime has also created an international Critical Information Infrastructure Protection (CIIP) Directory, various best practice documents, guides for computer and network security threat assessments, and the impact of such threats, both new and evolving, to law enforcement. In addition, the Subgroup has actively organized international training conferences for cybercrime agencies, conferences for law enforcement and industry on CIIP, and cooperation and tracing of criminal and terrorist communications, as well as negotiation on widely accepted principles and action plans to combat high-tech crime. [117]

3.5 World Customs Organization (WCO)

The World Customs Organization (WCO), recognized as the "voice of the global Customs community," is the only worldwide intergovernmental organization focused exclusively on customs matters. Its primary objectives are to develop global standards, to simplify and harmonize customs procedures, to facilitate international trade and supply chain security, to enhance customs enforcement and compliance activities, and to promote integrity and sustainable global customs capacity-building programs. [118] In particular, due to its role in facilitating global supply chain security, the WCO has taken an active role in promoting strategies on CIP and electronic crime.

The WCO Expert Group on Electronic Crime (ECEG), created in response to a recommendation by the 3rd Cybercrime Working Group in 2000[119], works under the WCO Enforcement Committee to "provide a specialist resource to the WCO to advise on aspects of electronic crime as it affects WCO members" and focuses on issues such as defense of electronic infrastructures, early warning of potential vulnerabilities, countering threats to core ICT competencies, keeping pace with new technologies, and providing recommendations for training and technological development. [120]

WCO partners with the EastWest Institute (EWI) every year to host its annual Worldwide Security Conference (WSC) in Brussels, Belgium. At the 5th WSC, recently held in February 2008, more than 700 high-level security experts from around the world gathered to assess key global security challenges, including cybercrime. Participants had the opportunity to attend a Cyber Crime session, at which moderators warned that "a cyber attack combined with a physical attack was the next level of threat" and recommended that there should be "a global sharing of information on emerging threats from extremist groups and cyber crimi-nals." [121]

3.6 International Incident Response

3.6.1 G8 24/7 Network of Contacts for High-Tech Crime

Created in 1997, the G8 24/7 Network of Contacts for High-Tech Crime was created to "enhance and supplement (but not replace) traditional methods of ob-taining assistance in cases involving networked communications and other related technologies," and is open to any nation wishing to join. The network, designed to allow participants to directly reach high-tech experts who are knowledgeable in computing and the collection of electronic evidence, is available at all hours, sev-en days a week, to receive information and/or requests for cooperation. [122] The driving force behind the network was the need to act on incidents of reported cy-bercrime across international borders quickly and efficiently, rather than through the traditional sluggish web of contacts for national law enforcement and interna-tional governance bodies. [123]

In an undated letter of invitation to countries, the network initially indicated some of its early successes, including the conviction of a murderer in the United Kingdom, facilitated by the preservation and disclosure of Internet records in the United States- as well as the aversion of hacking attempts on banks throughout the U.S., Germany, and Mexico. In the letter of invitation, the network also cited the ongoing investigation into the September 11, 2001, terrorist attacks as an example of how the lack of contact points in a particular country could impede the investi-gation of a serious threat. [124]

Although the 24/7 Network of Contacts for High-Tech Crime has shown suc-cess in the past with investigations and computer crimes that cross international borders, the G8 has not yet issued any official document or metric surveying its overall success, such as the total number of investigations or convictions attributed to the network. Aside from the few sources identified in this paper, no further in-formation about the network, including any recent activity or reference in the past several years, could be found.

3.7 International Law Enforcement Cooperation

International law enforcement agencies play an integral role in the protection of critical infrastructure and the enforcement of computer crime related laws. If a computer crime is committed within a nation's borders, most developed countries have the mechanisms and laws in place to appropriately stop the crime and prosecute the offender. However, since these crimes now increasingly cross national borders, the issue is greatly complicated for law enforcement agencies, which need the ability to quickly and efficiently share information, regardless of jurisdiction, and deploy appropriate forensic methods to collect evidence after a crime is committed. To date, most initiatives to coordinate law enforcement efforts continue to occur at the regional level.

3.7.1 International Criminal Police Organization (INTERPOL)

INTERPOL is the world's largest international police organization with 186 member countries. Created in 1923, it facilitates cross-border police cooperation, and supports and assists all organizations, authorities, and services whose mission is to prevent or combat international crime. Based in Europe, INTERPOL limits its involvement to crimes that occur in more than one member country. ICT crime, in particular, is handled as a sub-directorate under Financial and High Tech Crime.

Due to its size, INTERPOL operates through the use of Working Parties on IT Crime, which consist of the heads or experienced members of national computer crime units. These working parties have been designed to reflect regional expertise and exist in Europe, Asia-South Pacific, Latin America, Africa, and the Middle East and North Africa. In particular, the Working Parties have all shown a particular interest in training forensic teams in computer and electronic evidence collection. Current activities and accomplishments of each Working Party are described in more detail below, with the exception of the Middle East and North Africa Working Party, which is still in its early stages of development and has not yet been included on the INTERPOL Regional Working Parties website. [125]

The Steering Committee was formed to coordinate and harmonize the various regional working party initiatives and to facilitate communication between the working parties and other important ICT groups. It is represented by the Chairperson, Vice-Chairperson and a third member from each regional working party, and it is coordinated by a representative from the General Secretariat. [126] The Committee has worked with the G8 Subgroup on High-Tech Crime, the International Chamber of Commerce (ICC, see Chapter 5), the United Nations Office on

Drugs and Crime (UNODC), Europol (see Chapter 4), and several academic institutions on various information technology crime issues.

The European Working Party on Information Technology Crime's largest impact has been the production of its annually updated Information Technology Crime Investigation Manual (ITCIM), described on its website as "a best practice guide for the experienced [law enforcement] investigator, which is continually updated." [127] Recent updates to the IT Crime Manual include ongoing projects related to electronic means of payment, manipulation of public communications networks, criminal threats against e-commerce, tools and techniques, Internet investigations, and wireless technologies. The European Working Party's National Central Reference Points (NCRP) network is an international 24-hour response system containing a list of responsible experts in more than one hundred countries, which is currently expanding and has been endorsed by the G8 Subgroup on High-Tech Crime. As of August 2007, 111 INTERPOL National Bureaus have designated NCRPs.[128] In addition, EWPITC hosts numerous training courses for law enforcement members, including a recent Internet Investigations course in Tampere, Finland, in June 2007, and has been working on several projects related to botnets, malicious code, and Voice-over-IP (VoIP). [129]

In May 2005, INTERPOL held its 5th Meeting of the INTERPOL Working Party on IT Crime in Pretoria, Africa, at which delegates recommended the African Regional Working Party on Information Technology Crime take the lead on coordinating cybercrime training and awareness initiatives in Africa.[130] Since then, the African Working Party has been active in coordinating an awareness program to bring information on ICT crime regularly to top-level management in African countries. In addition, the Working Party has been committed to regional information sharing and capacity building initiatives, developing partnerships with other African organizations that deal with ICT crime, establishing best practices, enhancing information flow among regional Computer Crime Units, and promoting operating procedure standardization. [131]

The Asia-South Pacific Working Party on Information Technology Crime (ASPWP), established in 1997, holds annual meetings and numerous training workshops and seminars for member countries on cybercrime awareness, forensics, and investigations. At the 8th ASPWP meeting in Hong Kong, China, in December 2006, members agreed to begin new projects on investigative reference, 3G technologies, and mobile phone forensics. The last reported Working Party meeting was held in Bali, Indonesia, in November 2007, although no further information regarding the meeting could be found on the INTERPOL website. In addition to work on several other projects, such as intelligent scoping, case information sharing, training, and computer forensics, ASPWP has hosted several INTERPOL Information Technology Crime Investigation Seminars and Train-the-Trainer Workshops on Information Technology Crime Investigation and Computer Forensics for the Asia-South Pacific region. [132]

The Latin America Working Party on Information Technology Crime (LAWPITC), formed in 2005, also holds annual meetings for member countries. The aims of LAWPITC are similar to those of the other Working Parties, including international cooperation, promotion of standardization in procedures, and establishment of best practice guidelines. In practice, LAWPITC works to promote international police cooperation in Latin America, to share expertise on ICT crime investigation, and to supervise the work of subgroups specializing in high-tech crime in Latin American countries. The last Working Party meeting was held in Santiago, Chile, in March 2008, and the next meetings are scheduled for Spain and El Salvador later in 2008. [133]

Experts in law enforcement, academia, and the private sector gathered at the INTERPOL General Secretariat from September 19-20, 2005, for the 1st International Cybercrime Investigation Training Conference, involving more than seventy representatives from twenty countries. The attendees worked to address the areas of global harmonization of cybercrime training and institutions, finding additional qualified trainers, and engaging academia and private industry to support law enforcement's development and delivery of training modules. [134] The private sector also recognized INTERPOL's Training and Operational Standards Initiative for High-Tech Crime (TOPSI), which works through the INTERPOL Working Parties to "deliver strategic assessments, promote awareness, build capacity, create standards, and harmonize best practices" to support member countries.[135]

Law enforcement officials, security experts, and private sector representatives gathered with INTERPOL to discuss the latest developments in cybercrime at the 7th International Conference on Cyber-Crime in New Delhi, India, in September 2007. This followed prior conferences in Cairo, Egypt, in 2005, in Seoul, Korea, in 2002, and in Lyon, France, in 2000 and 1995. Key issues discussed at the 2007 conference included international cooperation, terrorist use of the Internet, online child exploitation, online banking fraud, and cyber-forensics. [136]

In addition to the various activities of the Regional Working Parties and international training conferences, INTERPOL also makes available several useful resources for individuals and businesses on the Information Technology Crime website, including technology descriptions and indications of potential criminality and suggested responses to cybercrime involving wireless and mobile technologies, multimedia messaging, and virtual money. [137] The website also offers practical tools on information security and crime prevention, including an explanatory report on IT Security and Crime Prevention for investigators, a Company Checklist for cybercrime prevention in the workplace, a list of frequently asked questions about IT security and crime prevention, and a private checklist for individuals to use to prevent misuse of IT systems. [138]

3.7.2 International Law Enforcement Telecommunications Seminar (ILETS)

ILETS, initiated by the United States Federal Bureau of Investigation (FBI) in 1993, is an annual gathering of law enforcement and national security agencies from a number of countries for cooperation on lawful telecommunications interception and data retention. The founding members are Australia, Canada, Hong Kong, United States and the United Kingdom plus Norway, Denmark, France, Germany, Netherlands, Spain, and Sweden.[139] The purpose of the group is to provide a cooperative forum, through which developments, issues, problems, and solutions in the area of lawful telecommunications interception and data retention can be considered and addressed. Issues are considered under the framework of the national laws of the attending agencies' respective countries and with regard to the protection of human and civil rights. Recommendations are reviewed by the respective governments to whom the agencies are ultimately responsible and, if accepted, they are adopted and implemented.[140]

One of the main issues discussed through ILETS is the International User Requirements (IUR) first put forward by the FBI in 1992 and later adopted by the European Union on January 17, 1995. These "Requirements" were released, in the name of the FBI and the Council of the European Union, for other countries to sign up to in November 1996. An attempt in 1998 to update the IURs in the European Union ("ENFOPOL 98") to cover mobile, satellite phones and Internet use was put on hold because of adverse public reaction. ILETS works directly with the Standards Technical Committee (STC) and its semi-public side is organized through the renamed "Policy and Legal Advisory Group" (PLAG).[141]

ILETS '99 was held in November 1999, in Saint Cyr au Mont d'Or, France. The topic of the seminar, later claimed to be sensitive to public and media attention, was "Reconciling data protection and privacy requirements in the 21st Century". On the issue of "data retention and implications of data protection legislation," the meeting agreed that, "all delegations [would] consider options for improving the retention of data by Communications Service Providers."[142] ILETS has also collaborated with the 3rd Generation Partnership Project (3GPP, see Chapter 5) and the ETSI Technical Committee on Lawful Interception (TC LI) (see Chapter 4) on related issues in recent years, according to meeting minutes from a 3GPP meeting held in Helsinki, Finland in September 2002.[143]

4 Regional Intergovernmental Organizations

While large international organizations such as the United Nations and OECD are currently pursuing global cyber security initiatives, a large amount of work is also being done by smaller, regional intergovernmental organizations. Regional organizations have the potential to make an impact because of their ability to relate to the needs of their smaller constituencies. However, because regional organizations frequently lack the funding and full support of member states, it is often a challenge to garner enough cooperation to make any recognizable impact on the global scale.

A majority of initiatives by regional intergovernmental organizations, aside from the work done by the Council of Europe on the Convention on Cybercrime, have been limited to providing resources to their member states and opening communication channels between nations. Cyber security policies and initiatives are in different forms and stages of implementation in different parts of the world. For example, the European region, with organizations such as the European Union, leads the way with regard to initiative success. Other organizations, such as APEC and the Organization of American States (OAS), are making similar progress in other regions around the world, such as Asia- Pacific and the Americas.

Although regional intergovernmental organizations in Africa and the Middle East have recently begun to show a greater interest in developing cyber security policy frameworks, training and awareness programs, and incident response capabilities, many of these activities still appear to be in a very early stage of development. Because many of the primary organizations with ICT security objectives in the Middle East, such as the League of Arab States and the Gulf Cooperation Council, do not offer extensive Arabic-English translation on their websites, these organizations have not been included in this section.

The following subsections include a breakdown of regional organizations currently active in the cyber security arena in Europe, Asia-Pacific, and the Americas, including a brief discussion on noteworthy activities dealing with intergovernmental policy implementation, harmonization of legal frameworks, cybercrime awareness, incident response, and law enforcement. Detailed analysis on the present state of cyber security in Africa is currently available in a separate ongoing study at Georgia Tech, accessible from the online Cyber Security Organization Catalog.

4.1 Europe

4.1.1 European Union (EU)

Established in 1993, the European Union is the largest governing body within Europe. The EU represents twenty-seven European countries and was established around three pillars: the European Communities, common foreign and security policy, and police and judicial cooperation in criminal manners.[144] In particular, the third pillar has enabled the European Union, through a series of Directives and Communications by the Commission of the European Communities ("the Commission"), to play a very active role in developing policy initiatives to combat cybercrime and promote a regional culture of cyber security in Europe since the 1990s.

The Information Society and Media Directorate General "supports the development and use of Information and Communication Technologies (ICTs) for the benefit of all citizens." Its role is to: "Support innovation and competitiveness in Europe through excellence in ICT research and development; define and implement a regulatory environment that enables rapid development of services based on information, communication and audio-visual technologies, so fostering competition that supports investment, growth and jobs; encourage the widespread availability and accessibility of ICT-based services, especially those that have the greatest impact on the quality of life of the citizens; foster the growth of content industries drawing on Europe's cultural diversity; and represent the European Commission in international dialogue and negotiations in these fields, and promote international cooperation in ICT research and development." [145]

Three committees of the European Parliament focus on the Information Society: The Committee on Industry, Research and Energy (ITRE); the Committee on Civil Liberties, Justice and Home Affairs (LIBE); and the Committee on Culture and Education (CULT). [146] ITRE is responsible for "the information society and information technology, including the establishment and development of trans-European networks in the telecommunication infrastructure sector." [147] Specific to information security, LIBE is responsible for "legislation in the areas of transparency and the protection of natural persons with regard to the processing of personal data." [148] CULT is responsible for the "audiovisual policy and the cultural and educational aspects of the information society." [149]

In March 1992, the European Council approved its first initial action in the field of security of information systems, establishing an action plan and a Senior Officials Committee.[150] In an early attempt to assess the landscape of cyber security in Europe, the Commission presented the results of a study on computer-related crime to the European Council in April 1998. In January 1999, the European Parliament and the Council approved a "multiannual action plan on promoting safer use of the Internet by combating illegal and harmful content on global networks." In October 1999 at the Tampere Summit, the European Council concluded that "high-tech crime should be included in the efforts to agree on common definitions and sanctions." In addition, the European Parliament called for commonly acceptable definitions for computer-related offences and the establishment of legislation in substantive criminal law.[151]

In January 2001, the Commission issued a Communication on *Creating a Safer Information Society by Improving the Security of Information Infrastructures and Combating Computer-related Crime*, which defined computer crime and proposed legislative and non-legislative provisions to deal with domestic and transnational cybercrime activities.[152] Shortly after, in June 2001, the Commission issued another related Communication on *Network and Information Security: Proposal for a European Policy Approach*, recommending awareness raising, a European warning and information system, support for technology and market-oriented standardization, a legal framework, security in government use, and international cooperation.[153] As part of an initial effort to adopt a strategy on combating high-tech crime, the Commission encouraged Member States to join the G8 24/7 Network of Contacts for High-Tech Crime (G8, see Chapter 3).[154] In 2002, the Commission issued a proposal for a Council *Framework Decision on attacks against information systems*, which would create a "common set of legal definitions and criminal offenses across the EU" and require Member States to join the G8 24/7 Network.[155]

The European Council adopted resolutions *2002/C 43/02: On a Common Approach and specific actions in the area of networks and Information Security* and *2003/C 48/01: On a European approach towards a culture of network and information security* to stress the need for a comprehensive European strategy to "strive towards a culture of security, taking into account the importance of international cooperation." [156] [157] In June 2003, the European Parliament and the Council further extended the original multiannual Safe Internet Action Plan from 1999 through 2004, again in May 2005 as "Safe Internet *plus*" through 2008,[158] and recently proposed to extend it again in February 2008 as "Safer Internet Programme" through 2013.[159]

The Council adopted a *Directive on Privacy and Electronic Communications* in July 2002 and the *Framework Decision on attacks against information systems* in February 2005 to address spyware-related activities like illegal access and interference with information systems.[160] The Council adopted Directive 2002/58/EC in July 2002 to address "the processing of personal data and the protection of privacy in the electronic communications sector." Specifically, this directive ensures that communications cannot be stored or otherwise used without the user's consent. Users must be given the opportunity to refuse through an opt-in approach that applies to cookies, public directories, and spamming. [161]

The eEurope Action Plan, launched in its first phase at the European Council meeting in Seville in 2002 and endorsed by the Council of Ministers in the eEurope Resolution of January 2003, was created to "develop modern public services and a dynamic environment for e-business through widespread availability of broadband access at competitive prices and a secure information infrastructure." As one of the Action Plan's six policy priorities and a key component of the Commission's vision for the Next Generation Internet, security would be addressed through measures like the electronic signatures directive, data protection legislation for electronic communications, enhanced network and information security, and secure communications for eGovernment.[162] Several other initiatives were also proposed, including the creation of ENISA (see below), the Network and Information Security (NIS) Focus Group, and eTEN (Trans-European Networks for Telecommunications),[163] as well as an Information Technology Risk Preparedness Survey for European firms[164] and a Handbook of Legislative Procedures of Computer and Network Misuse for European CSIRTs.[165] Following success of the eEurope Action Plan in 2005, the Commission launched *Communication: i2010 – A European Information Society for growth and employment* "as a framework for addressing the main challenges and developments in the information society and media sectors up to 2010." [166]

The Commission issued a Communication in May 2006 on *A strategy for a Secure Information Society – "Dialogue, partnership, and empowerment,"* which identified a "change in the threat landscape" and highlighted the need for a multi-stakeholder approach in identifying and meeting new security challenges in relation to information systems and networks in the EU. The 2006 Commission also set forth a comprehensive strategy to embrace specific network and information security measures, a regulatory framework for electronic communications, and the fight against cybercrime. In support of this strategy, the EU consulted several professional services organizations in April 2007 to survey the availability and robustness of European electronic communication networks. [167]

In May 2007, the Commission issued a Communication *Towards a general policy on the fight against cyber crime* as an update to the 2001 Communication. The 2007 Communication was also supported by an external study conducted by a third party management consulting firm via interviews with relevant stakeholders (such as Commission officials, law enforcement bodies, national prosecutors, ISPs, private industry, network and information security associations, and academia). The study results indicated a global consensus among stakeholders regarding the EU's need for a general policy on combating cybercrime. [168]

The 2007 Communication cited numerous plans and recommendations to aid in the fight against cybercrime, including a Commission agreement to organize at least one expert meeting in 2007 dedicated to further public-private cooperation and to consider setting up a central EU cybercrime contact point. In addition, the Commission agreed to develop an EU cybercrime training platform in order to co-ordinate all multinational training efforts in the field. In an effort to combat illegal content, the Communication recommended the development of "EU-level volun-tary agreements and conventions between public authorities and private operators, especially ISPs, regarding procedures to block and close down illegal Internet sites." The Commission also intended to implement an in-depth analysis of iden-tity theft to assist with the preparation of specific EU legislation. Lastly, the Communication strongly encouraged all Member States to ratify the Council of Europe's Convention on Cybercrime and its additional protocol. [169]

Through the Community Research and Development Information Service (CORDIS) Seventh Research Framework Programme (FP7) in 2007-2008, the EU is also developing numerous research programs, reports, publications, and metrics on ICT trust and security, secure network infrastructures, identity management, and critical infrastructure protection. [170]

The EU has also placed considerable emphasis on the fight against spam. In 2002, the EU adopted the *Directive on Privacy and Electronic Communication* to officially ban spam. Subsequently, the Commission has focused on the areas of "awareness, self-regulation/technical actions, cooperation and enforcement." [171] In 2002, the Commission created the Contact Network of Spam Authorities (CNSA) in an effort to share information on current spam fighting practices with national authorities. These current practices included suggested methods for re-ceiving and handling complaint information and intelligence, as well as investiga-tive and countermeasure techniques.[172] Following another Communication in early 2004- *On unsolicited commercial communications or 'spam,'* [173] the Com-mission, in collaboration with OECD (see Chapter 3), hosted a workshop on spam and has actively contributed to the Anti-Spam Toolkit, which provides a "compre-hensive package of regulatory approaches, technical solutions, and industry initia-tives to fight spam." [174]

Despite these efforts, however, the Commission concluded in its November 2006 Communication *On Fighting spam, spyware, and malicious software* that improvement was still needed in anti-spam enforcement efforts, actions by indus-try, and cooperation at the national level, both within government and between government and industry. Going forward, the Commission intended to further its cooperation efforts, examine the opportunity to make new legislative proposals, and undertake research actions to strengthen privacy and security in the e-Communication sector. The Commission agreed to monitor the implementation of these actions and provide an assessment of any necessary additional actions in 2008.[175]

4.1.2 Council of Europe (COE)

The Council of Europe was founded in 1949 "to develop throughout Europe common and democratic principles based on the European Convention on Human Rights and other reference texts on the protection of individuals." As of March 2008, the Council of Europe is comprised of forty-seven member countries, one applicant country, and five "observer" countries (including the United States, Japan, Mexico, Canada, and the Holy See).[176] Through promotion of the Convention on Cybercrime (described in greater detail in Chapter 2), the Council seeks to "pursue a common criminal policy aimed at the protection of society against cybercrime, especially by adopting appropriate legislation and fostering international cooperation." [177]

While the majority of recent cyber security initiatives by the Council of Europe have focused on the Convention on Cybercrime, the Council has also called on the need for a secure Information Society in the fight against terrorism and organized crime, the protection of children against sexual exploitation and sexual abuse, and the protection of human rights and fundamental freedoms, including the protection of personal data. [178]

In December 2005, the Council of Europe hosted a conference on "Cybercrime: a Global Challenge, a Global Response," in cooperation with the Ministry of Justice of Spain and the Organization of American States (OAS, see next subsection) in Madrid, Spain, encouraging OAS member states to recognize the global scope of cybercrime and to pursue international cooperation and technical assistance in adopting appropriate legislation and implementing appropriate training to combat cybercrime.[179] In early 2006, the Council of Europe made public a report detailing trends in organized crime in 2005, including facts, figures, and trends on organized criminal activities in Europe, such as those involving cybercrime.[180]

The Council of Europe organized several regional and international workshops and conferences on emerging cyber security issues, such as data privacy, identity theft, freedom of information, and cybercrime legislation in 2007. More than 140 cybercrime experts from around the world met at the Council of Europe "Octopus Interface conference on Cooperation against cybercrime" in Strasbourg, France, in June 2007 to analyze the threat of cybercrime, review the effectiveness of cybercrime legislation, and promote multi-stakeholder cooperation.[181] In October 2007, the Council of Europe assisted the Philippines' GRP-Department of Justice and the Commission on Information Communication Technology in hosting a "Legislators and Experts Workshop on Cybercrime" at which a draft national cybercrime bill was under discussion and review at the time for endorsement by stakeholders.[182]

On November 7, 2007, the Council of Europe adopted *Recommendation CM/Rec(2007)16 of the Committee of Ministers to member states on measures to promote the public service value of the Internet*, calling on the governments of member states to uphold human rights, democracy, and rule of law on the Internet, elaborating and delineating stakeholder roles and responsibilities, and encouraging the private sector to acknowledge and familiarize itself with its evolving ethical roles and responsibilities and to develop new forms of open and transparent self- and co-regulation.[183] Together with OSCE (see below) and the United Nations Educations, Scientific and Cultural Organization (UNESCO) the Council held a workshop in Rio de Janeiro, Brazil, on freedom of expression as a security issue. In particular, the workshop "emphasized the need for the industry's Internet content management to comply fully with human rights standards, particularly with regard to the right to freedom of expression and information regardless of frontiers." [184]

In November 2007, the Council of Europe also held two conferences dealing with cybercrime and identity theft, the first in Portugal ("European Conference on identity fraud and theft")[185] and the second in Courmayeur, Italy ("Identity Theft and the Convention on Cybercrime").[186] Conference participants collaborated to define criminalization of identity theft and potential avenues for implementing legislative frameworks for criminal offenses.

On November 27, 2007, in Cairo, Egypt, hundreds of representatives from government, the private sector, and non-governmental organizations from the Arab region and other countries participated in the first regional conference on cybercrime, hosted by the Council of Europe, and established the "Cairo Declaration against Cybercrime." Participants at the conference agreed to strengthen cybercrime legislation and investigations and to consider creating Computer Emergency Response Teams (CERTs, see Chapter 5) in the Arab region. In addition, Arab countries agreed to adopt legislation and provide hotlines and prosecution services to protect against sexual exploitation and abuse of children on the Internet, and encourage regional and international cooperation through private-public partnerships. [187]

In December 2007, the Council of Europe held a regional workshop on cybercrime legislation and training of judges in Plovdiv, Bulgaria, to review regional cybercrime legislation, investigation and prosecution of cybercrime, international cooperation, electronic evidence, and training of judges on forensic cybercrime investigation and prosecution.[188] The Council also hosted a conference in Strasbourg, France, in early April 2008 to reinforce the fight against Internet-based crimes by inviting experts from around the world, as well as representatives from governments, police forces, and the Internet industry. At the conference, participants had the opportunity to review the effectiveness of current cybercrime legislation and adopt new guidelines on forging formal partnerships between Internet Service Providers (ISPs) and law enforcement.[189]

The Council of Europe also recently hosted Octopus Interface 2008 in Strasbourg, France, from April 1-2, 2008, at which more than 200 cybercrime experts from 65 countries, international organizations, and the private sector met to discuss current and emerging cybercrime threats (including malware, identity theft, botnets, denial of service attacks, and attacks against VoIP and NGN), the effectiveness of cybercrime legislation, measures to enhance the effectiveness of international cooperation, adopted guidelines for cooperation between law enforcement and Internet Service Providers (ISPs) in the investigation of cybercrime, and the need to ensure a balance between the need for security and the protection of individual privacy. [190]

Beyond 2008, the Council of Europe intends to continue pursuing regional and international cooperation with both public and private organizations committed to strengthening cybercrime legislation and capacities for cybercrime investigation and prosecution. [191] The Council is also planning numerous workshops, conferences, and meetings around the world, including the Counter eCrime Operations Summit (CeCOS) II in Tokyo, Japan, in May 2008.[192]

4.1.3 Organization for Security and Co-operation in Europe (OSCE)

The Organization for Security and Co-operation in Europe (OSCE) is the world's largest security organization, consisting of fifty-six states in Europe, Central Asia, and America.[193] In 2002, the OSCE established the Action Against Terrorism Unit (ATU) to "coordinat[e] and facilitat[e] … OSCE initiatives and capacity-building programmes relevant to the struggle against terrorism." [194] The Bucharest Plan of Action, the ATU's political framework for fighting terrorism, includes mandates for "combating the use of the Internet for terrorist purposes" and "enhancing legal co-operation in criminal matters to counter-terrorism." [195]

The ATU organized workshops in 2005 and 2006 which provided a means to exchange best practices and encourage international legal cooperation. The ATU also organized "national training workshops for prosecutors, judges and judicial officials on issues of extradition and mutual legal assistance in criminal matters, in particular those related to terrorism." These workshops were created to respond to the growing concern on the exploitation of the Internet by terrorists, "including its use to identify and attract new recruits, to collect and transfer funds, to organize terrorist acts and to incite the commission of terrorist offences in particular through the use of propaganda." [196]

At the December 2006 OSCE Ministerial Council Meeting, the Council passed decision *7/06: Countering the Use of the Internet for Terrorist Purposes,* which called for states to expand international cooperation, take appropriate measures to protect critical infrastructures, increase monitoring of terrorist websites, and adopt the CoE Convention on Cybercrime. The decision, which served as an update to existing decision *3/04: Combating the Use of the Internet for Terrorist Purposes,*[197] also encouraged member states to participate in the G8 24/7 Network of Contacts for High-Tech Crime [198] and to attend the Conference on Public-Private Partnerships in combating terrorism. Held in May 2007, the Conference urged cooperation and collaboration between states and private industry to enhance critical infrastructure protection and support the fight against terrorism.[199]

At the 2007 OSCE Expert Workshop on Combating Incitement to Terrorism on the Internet, participants were able to link themes from previous workshops in discussing the "…areas of combating the use of the Internet for terrorist purposes and in the area of fighting incitement to terrorism and related terrorist activities." In a speech to the Second Information Security Forum in Garmisch, Germany, on April 10, 2008, Raphael Perl, Head of the OSCE Action against Terrorism Unit, warned about a recent rise in terrorist use of the Internet and the possible threat of using the Internet for cyber attacks alongside attacks on physical targets. According to Perl, "the private sector is our most natural ally in combating the use of Internet for terrorist purposes. More needs to be done as well for the development of an active, educated, and vigilant civil society, which is essential for effective counter-terrorism measures regarding cyberspace." [200]

4.1.4 European Telecommunications Standards Institute (ETSI)

The European Commission has recognized the European Telecommunications Standards Institute (ETSI) as a European Standards Organization. ETSI is a not-for-profit organization that "produces globally-applicable standards for Information and Communications Technology (ICT), including fixed, mobile, radio, converged, broadcast and internet technologies." [201] In particular, ETSI has contributed numerous ICT security standards to the Information Society in the past few years, including standardization of mobile and wireless security, cryptographic algorithms, smart cards, Next Generation Networks, lawful interception (LI), electronic signatures, and proofing products against crime.[202]

Since 2006, ETSI has hosted annual Security Workshops in Sophia-Antipolis, France, which bring together security standards experts from around the world. At the 2006 "ETSI Future Security Workshop: The threats, risks, and opportunities," the group identified the following topics as being of vital importance: Next Generation Networks, definition of privacy levels, product proofing, collaboration with standards bodies, digital rights management, X.805, Common Criteria and TVRA, Data Retention Directive, network issues, mobile terminal security, security in banking systems, and real-time security challenges.[203]

At the "ETSI 2nd Security Workshop: Future Security" in 2007, security experts gathered from organizations such as The European Commission, ITU-T, ENISA, ISO/IEC, and others, and identified the following key issues: product proofing, regulation modeling, smart cards, ITU network of experts, smart card high speed interface, public warning systems, Data Rights Management (DRM), authentication architecture in 3G, healthcare, and identity management.[204] A 3rd ETSI Security Workshop was held in January 2008, which included sessions on mobile security, security initiatives within CEN (see below), lawful interception, new security challenges, smart cards, international standardization, Next Generation Networks (NGN) security, and cryptography.[205]

4.1.5 European Committee for Standardization (CEN)

The European Committee for Standardization (CEN) is a non-profit technical organization supporting the objectives of the European Union and the European Economic Area by promoting standards in free trade, safety of workers and consumers, interoperability of networks, environmental protection, exploitation of research and development programs, and public procurement.[206] Through the various activities, focus groups, technical committees, and workshops of CEN/ISSS (Information Society Standardization System), CEN has done much to contribute to the Information Society throughout Europe. In particular, CEN/ISSS has provided significant work on security, trust, and data protection through completed focus groups on eBusiness, e-Invoicing, digital rights management (DRM), network and information security (NIS), and eHealth, as well as current focus groups on biometrics, eGovernment, and cultural diversity.[207] In addition, CEN/ISSS is currently working on the second phase of a Data Protection and Privacy Workshop, Anti-Counterfeiting: Protocols for Detection of Counterfeits, a Cyber ID Workshop, and Information System for Disaster and Emergency Management.[208]

In response to the European Council's 2001 Communication on *Network and Information Security: proposal for a European policy approach* and the European Council's 2002 Resolution *On a common approach and specific actions in the area of network and information security*, the CEN/ISSS Network and Information Security Focus Group, in collaboration with ETSI (see above), released a Final Report in October 2003 which addressed "standardization activities and standardization requirements with respect to Network and Information Security." [209] The report contained detailed recommendations and information on "relevant existing and developing standards that contribute to Network and Information Security and support the requirement for interoperability in a global e-business environment." [210] Subsequent revisions to this report were later completed in 2006 by the ICT Standards Board's Network and Information Security Steering Group (ICTSB/NISSG, see below). [211]

4.1.6 ICT Standards Board (ICTSB)

The Information and Communication Technologies Standards Board (ICTSB) is a "collaborative group of organizations concerned with standardization and related activities in information and communications technologies," and its principal objective is to support an effective standardization system in Europe through various project teams and working groups. ICTSB's three primary members include ETSI, CEN, and the European Committee for Electrotechnical Standardization (CENELEC). [212] The primary contribution of ICTSB to the global cyber security initiative has been through its Network and Information Security Steering Group (NISSG), which was created in March 2004 to take over work on the CEN/ISSS NIS Focus Group's Final Report (see above). Working together with ENISA (see below) between 2006 and 2007, NISSG helped facilitate the report's standardization requirements and produced a revised version in March 2007. Following production of the updated report, NISSG and ENISA joined with ITU-T Study Group 17 (see Chapter 3) in a collaborative effort to make available online the report's standards and specifications. [213]

In the NIS Standards Final Report, published in June 2007, technology ("diversity, openness, and interoperability"), people ("culture of security and trust"), and best practices ("information security management") are the key issues central to the report's recommendations. The recommendations focus on registration, authentication, and authorization services, confidentiality and privacy services, trust services, network and information security management systems and services, and assurance services. The existing standards identified in the report are listed in a database on the ITU-T Study Group 17's website which allows "an interactive search for standards dealing with particular security topics and for standards that have been issued by a specific standards body." [214]

In addition to work on the NIS Standards Report, NISSG also provides other information and resources on its website, including information on current technical activities, links to EC initiatives, and other interesting links related to network and information security.[215] In January 2007, NISSG joined ENISA and ITU-T Study Group 17 in developing the ICT Security Standards Roadmap, designed to "[aid] the process of standards development...[and] provide information that will help potential users of security standards, and other standards stakeholders, gain an understanding of what standards are available or under development as well as the key organizations that are working on these standards." The five parts of the Roadmap, which is still a work in progress, include ICT standards development organizations and their work, approved ICT security standards, security standards under development, future needs and proposed new security standards, and best practices. [216]

4.1.7 European Network and Information Security Agency (ENISA)

In 2004, the European Union formed the European Network and Information Security Agency (ENISA), a designated Center of Excellence on Network and Information Security (NIS), to "enhance the capability of the Community, the Member States and the business community to address and respond to network and information security problems." [217] The agency is focused on three primary areas: awareness-raising, communication between members, and data collection and prevention. The agency's *Users Guide: How to Raise Information Security Awareness* was designed to illustrate simple strategies on how to plan, organize, and run an information security awareness program. ENISA also serves as a central data storage group for security incidents and other emerging risks within Europe and has a central role in coordinating communication between regional CERTs. [218]

In accordance with its Work Programme in 2006, ENISA produced an inventory and updated map of European Computer Security Incident Response Teams (CSIRT, see Chapter 5), created a step-by-step manual on how to set up a CSIRT, and released the document *CERT cooperation and its further facilitation by the relevant stakeholders*." [219] The agency also updated and improved its "Who is Who" Directory of Network and Information Security players in Europe, the "User's Guide to Awareness Raising," and the Awareness Raising Information Package. Additionally, ENISA created an inventory of methods, tools, and best practices in Risk Management and delivered two studies on anti-spam measures, which indicated a need for incentives to encourage providers to contribute to the overall security of interconnected networks.[220]

The EU commissioned an external review of ENISA in 2006 to assess its effectiveness, which determined that "the agency is respecting its work programme, but its achievements, while adequate or even good so far, appear insufficient to achieve the high level of impacts and value added hoped for." Although the Panel of Experts did identify several strengths, including the political mandate by the Commission, the development of relationships and networks at the EU level, and the competence of the staff, it also identified numerous weaknesses, including a "lack of vision and focus in the implementation of the mission of the agency, as well as a lack of flexibility in the work organisation." The agency's location in Crete and the inadequate size of its operational staff were also perceived as constraints on the efficiency of networking activities and human resources recruitment and management. Despite these weaknesses, however, the Panel of Experts determined that the closure of ENISA "would represent a relevant missed opportunity for Europe" and recommended the renewal of its Mandate beyond 2009.[221]

In 2007, ENISA implemented a new website to tackle Emerging Risks, promoted its Awareness Raising Guide internationally, presented a study on the Collection and Dissemination of Information, related to Emerging Risks in the area of Information Technology, worked with the ITU to develop a new single-point online portal on IT security standards for all of Europe, presented a Legal Overview in Risk Management for business and security experts, presented the first report on current EU practices and assessing the success of information security awareness raising activities, launched its first position paper – *15 key threats and 19 recommendations for safer social networking* – and a paper on Botnets, calling for "stronger persecution of cyber criminals to combat 6 million computers, silently hijacked for online fraud." [222]

The ENISA Work Programme for 2008 ("Build on Synergies: Achieve Impact") "…is the result of a new, closer consultation process with all stakeholders" and focuses on three multi-annual thematic programs: (1) improving resilience in European e-Communication networks, (2) developing and maintaining cooperation models, and (3) identifying emerging risks for creating trust and confidence. In addition, the agency is planning a "preparatory action" on micro enterprises, focusing on their needs and expectations in NIS. [223]

4.1.8 European Incident Response

4.1.8.1 European Task Force on Computer Security Incident Response Teams (TF-CSIRT)

The European Task Force on Computer Security Incident Response Teams is one of TERENA's task forces and represents major initiatives by the European region with regard to Computer Security Incident Response Teams (CSIRTs, see Chapter 5) creation and communication. TF-CSIRT provides a forum where members of the European Union and neighboring countries can exchange CSIRT experiences and knowledge in a secure environment. Established in 1999, and renewed again in June 2006, TF-CSIRT is actively involved in establishing new CSIRTs and CSIRT-related initiatives within the European community through the promotion of common standards and procedures for responding to computer security incidents. In addition, TF-CSIRT believes that common standards can decrease the response time associated with computer security incidents within its region. [224]

TF-CSIRT encourages cooperation throughout Europe through seminars, conferences, and a variety of different CSIRT-related services. The Task Force offers a CSIRT Starter Kit and has designed a mentoring scheme where more developed CSIRTs can mentor recently established CSIRTs. Additionally, the Task Force offers training for new CSIRT staff, an Internet resource contact database, and a variety of incident handling security guides and tools,[225] such as the Request Tracker for Incident Response (RTIR)- "a tool supporting CSIRTs in their daily work, registering incidents and keeping track of the workflow in handling an incident." [226] Finally, TF-CSIRT offers a rigorous accreditation service for European CSIRTs, including recent creation of the Trusted Introducer (TI) system, which provides an accreditation program to increase the level of trust between CSIRTs. [227]

From 2002-2005, TF-CSIRT coordinated the TRANSITS program to promote the establishment and enhancement of CSIRTs by addressing the problem of the shortage of skilled CSIRT staff. By providing training courses through the program, it attempted to train new staff for CSIRTs in organization, operational, technical, and legal issues framed around CSIRTs. The primary outcome of this project was the creation of training course materials for future CSIRTs and, since the end of the project, ENISA and FIRST (see Chapter 5) have co-organized several subsequent training sessions with TF-CSIRT. [228] The 24th TF-CSIRT Meeting was held in Oslo, Norway, in May 2008.

4.1.9 European Law Enforcement Cooperation

4.1.9.1 European Law Enforcement Organisation (Europol)

Europol, fully established in 1999, is the European Union's criminal intelligence agency. As of 2008, Europol covers all twenty-seven member-states of the European Union and serves as a liaison between the police forces of all member countries. Europol's aim is "to improve the effectiveness and cooperation between the competent authorities of the member states primarily by sharing and pooling intelligence to prevent and combat serious international organized crime," and its mission is "to make a significant contribution to the European Union's law enforcement efforts targeting organized crime." [229]

Europol's primary contribution to cybercrime prevention was the creation of The Europol Computer System (TECS), deployed in 2005 to facilitate sharing and analysis of criminal data between EU members and law enforcement organizations in other countries. Each EU Member Nation has assigned two Data Protection Experts to Europol to closely monitor how personal data is stored and used. Since its release, however, TECS has been highly scrutinized for how data is collected and stored within the system. There have been concerns as to the security of data stored in the system and other issues related to data protection. Since the system holds sensitive data, there have been concerns regarding data mining, as well as the trust placed in data imported from other countries and third parties. [230]

In August 2007, the Europol High-Tech Crime Centre released *High-Tech Crimes Within the EU: Threat Assessment 2007*, seen as a "tool to support the fight against high tech crime in a proactive way." In identifying the newest computer security threats most significant at the time, Europol highlighted the impact of criminal organizations in high tech crimes, botnets and crimewares, phishing/pharming/vishing/SMiShing, identity theft, cyber terrorism, drug trafficking and trafficking of child pornography on the Internet, and critical information infrastructures. [231] Europol also released an *EU Terrorism Situation and Trend Report* in 2007 describing the present context of terrorism in the EU, including numerous references to the challenge of identifying right-wing and Islamist terrorists based on propaganda disseminated on the Internet. According to the report, "the Internet is used by terrorists in various ways for both internal and external communications. Virtually all types of terrorist groups have [now] gone online." [232]

4.1.9.2 National Policing Improvement Agency (NPIA)

The National Policing Improvement Agency was created in 2007 to support police force operations throughout Europe. In particular, NPIA has a division dedicated to High Tech Crime, with programs designed "to ensure that police staff are equipped with the knowledge and skills to meet the challenges set by criminals who use technology unlawfully." With a heavy focus on training and education in cybercrime for law enforcement, NPIA offers a Masters in Cybercrime Forensics program and a First Responder e-Learning course for interested officers, as well as a diverse set of related courses on Internet forensics, network investigations, mobile phone forensics, identifying and tracing electronic suspects, and the role of technology in child abuse and economic crime investigations. [233]

NPIA also hosts frequent conferences and workshops on high tech crime for national and international law enforcement agencies. The ACPO e-Crime Conference is currently scheduled for June 25-27, 2008 in Wyboston, England, and a High Tech Crime Search and Seizure workshop is being planned for November 6-7, 2008. In addition, a Peer Precision course for "training on free software to assist in tracing and locating individuals who possess abusive images of children" is also currently planned for 2008. [234]

48

4.2 Asia-Pacific

4.2.1 Asia-Pacific Economic Cooperation (APEC)

The primary organization responsible for facilitating economic growth, cooperation, trade, and investment in the Asia-Pacific region is the Asia-Pacific Economic Cooperation (APEC). Established in 1989, the organization promotes economic growth and integration in the Pacific Rim and is composed of twenty-one members. APEC focuses its efforts on trade and investment liberalization, business facilitation, and economic and technical cooperation. [235]

APEC's Working Groups perform work in specific sectors as directed by the APEC Economic Leaders, Ministers, Sectoral Ministers, and Senior Officials. The Telecommunications and Information Working Group (TEL) was formed in 1990 and "aims to improve telecommunications and information infrastructure in the Asia-Pacific region by developing and implementing appropriate telecommunications and information policies, including relevant human resource and development cooperation strategies." TEL's priorities, as determined by the Telecommunications and Information Ministers and Leaders (TELMIN), include a focus on the protection of information and communications infrastructure and cyber security. The Security and Prosperity Steering Group, a subgroup of TEL, works specifically towards this purpose. [236]

In 2002, TEL issued the Shanghai Declaration, which included a *Statement on the Security of Information and Communications Infrastructures* and a Program of Action (APEC's Cyber-Security Strategy). The strategy identified six areas that serve as the basis for APEC's efforts on cybercrime and critical infrastructure protection: legal developments, information sharing and cooperation, security and technical guidelines, public awareness, training and education, and wireless security. The strategy encouraged member economies to work with APEC to develop and adopt "comprehensive substantive, procedural, and mutual assistance laws and policies," paying close attention to the Convention on Cybercrime. Member economies were also encouraged to develop institutions, such as CERTs (see Chapter 5), to facilitate the exchange of threat and vulnerability assessments. Further, the strategy strongly recommended that members join the G8 Network of Contacts for High-Tech Crime (see Chapter 3). In order to assist governments and corporations in the fight against cybercrime, the strategy encouraged that ICT security standards and best practices be identified and focused specifically on legal and policy issues related to encryption, PKI, and the authentication of electronic transactions. [237]

The 2002 Program of Action encouraged member economies to leverage work developed by other international organizations to improve regional public awareness regarding cyber security. These awareness-raising practices could include promotional and outreach materials, a catalogue of ongoing efforts, and a listserv or website to provide information on cyber ethics and cyber-responsibility. In order to improve the quality of human resources, the 2002 Program of Action declared as critical training opportunities on technical, forensic, and legal issues of cybercrime. Training and education efforts are to be focused on technology security professionals and professional-qualification certification schemes.[238]

TEL holds semi-annual meetings to discuss the status of cyber security in the Asia-Pacific region. At TEL meetings, the Security and Prosperity Steering Group (SPSG) provides an update of the status of specific items from its ongoing and recently completed projects. The Steering Group is also currently in the process of developing an online portal and Information Security Certification Awareness Program (or "Buyer's Guide") to raise awareness of public and private sector management. In addition, the International PKI and e-Authentication Training project was recently approved, and a training program took place in September 2007. The goal of the program was to increase PKI/e-Authentication implementation and promote PKI/e-Authentication awareness, as well as to strengthen the capabilities of Regulators. [239]

At the 6th APEC TELMIN meeting in Lima, Peru, in June 2005, TELMIN adopted *APEC Principles and Implementation Guidelines for Action against Spam* and *Guiding Principles for PKI-based Approaches to Electronic Authentication*. The spam guidelines addressed actions to be taken by government, anti-spam agencies, industry, and consumers, and contained suggestions such as the designation of a responsible agency with domestic and international authority, international cooperation with existing anti-spam agencies, and education and awareness activities. [240] The PKI guidelines focused on certificate registration and validation, key management, directory standards, and management guidelines. [241]

In April 2007, APEC collaborated with OECD (see Chapter 3) to host a workshop on malware at the 35th APEC TEL meeting in Manila, Philippines. The workshop focused on coordination with other national and international organizations, policies to address the issue, and capabilities and counter measures to respond to cyber attacks. APEC also co-hosted a workshop on network security with ASEAN (see below), focusing on cybercrime legislation, policy, and regulatory and enforcement capacity building. In addition, China introduced a "Guide on Policy and Technical Approaches against Botnets" to promote information exchange and discussion on botnets among APEC members. Several other initiatives were also proposed, including a workshop on cyber security and CIIP exercises in October 2007 that would focus on the "value of exercises in establishing, testing, and improving communications and cyber incident response as well as sharing best practices for successful exercises." [242]

APEC hosted TEL36 in October 2007, in Santiago, Chile, at which the Steering Group proposed several new projects and workshops, including Telecommunications for Disaster Management and Best Practices, Handheld Mobile Device Security, and Building confidence towards the trusted ICT society with ICT products and services. [243] At the 37th APEC TEL meeting in Tokyo, Japan, in March 2008, the Steering Group presented workshops on Policy and Technical Approaches against Botnets, ICT Products/Services Security, and Handheld Mobile Devices Security.[244] TEL38 is currently scheduled for October 2008 in Lima, Peru.[245]

TEL is also currently working with the APEC Counter Terrorism Task Force (CTTF) on issues related to cyber terrorism. In November 2007, the two groups co-hosted a Seminar on Protection of Cyberspace from Terrorist Use and Attack in South Korea.[246] In addition, TEL is working with the private sector to identify new technologies and challenges related to Next Generation Networks (NGN), including initiatives on e-commerce, e-government, e-security, disaster preparation, online learning, and skills standards development. [247]

4.2.2 Association of Southeast Asian Nations (ASEAN)

The goals of the Association of Southeast Asian Nations (ASEAN) are to "accelerate economic growth, social progress, and cultural development in the region and to promote regional peace and stability through abiding respect for justice and the rule of law in the relationship among countries in the region and adherence to the principles of the United Nations Charter." [248] ASEAN states that its vision is to "meet the ever increasing demand for improved infrastructure and communications by developing an integrated and harmonized trans-ASEAN transportation network and harnessing technology advances in telecommunication and information technology, especially in linking the planned information highways/multimedia corridors in ASEAN, promoting open sky policy, developing multi-modal transport, facilitating goods in transit and integrating telecommunications networks through greater interconnectivity, coordination of frequencies and mutual recognition of equipment-type approval procedures." [249]

4.2.2.1 ASEAN Regional Forum (ARF)

The ASEAN Regional Forum (ARF) organizes an annual Seminar on Cyber Terrorism. Previous seminars have focused on such topics as assessing the implications of cyber terrorism on national and global security, private-government partnerships, creation of CSIRTs (see Chapter 5), harmonization of domestic laws and regulations, and the enhancement of cooperation amongst members.[250] At the

4th ASEAN Regional Forum Seminar on Cyber Terrorism in Busan, Korea, in October 2007, ARF presented "mechanisms for coping with cyber terrorism..., measures to protect major national infrastructure, and ways to promote regional cooperation in the cyber security sector." The seminar also promoted the understanding of threat by cyber terrorism among the ARF member countries, encouraged "regional cooperation in systematically and institutionally coping with cyber terrorism," and approved a Conference on Terrorist Use of the Internet to be scheduled for the second half of 2008. [251] [252]

In accordance with the 2006 13th ARF *Statement on Cooperation in Fighting Cyber Attack and Terrorist Misuse of Cyberspace*, in which participants agreed to "identify national cyber-security units and increase coordination among national agencies... and joining or participating in established networks of cooperation," members at the 4th ARF Seminar on Cyber Terrorism agreed to create a Virtual Working Group (VWG) on Cyber Security and Cyber Terrorism. The primary tasks of the ARF Virtual Working Group, which would work and/or consult through virtual meetings, are "to take forward substantial cooperation in specific areas of cyber security and terrorism... and to strengthen the response capacity of the participating states by facilitating the real time exchange of information on threat and vulnerability assessments, identifying capacity-building needs, and providing practical recommendations." [253]

4.2.2.2 ASEAN Telecommunications and IT Ministers (TELMIN)

The Telecommunications and IT Ministers of ASEAN (TELMIN) focuses mainly on building capacity and cooperation relating to ICT. TELMIN's work is largely completed through the ASEAN Telecommunications Regulators Council (ATRC) and the ASEAN Telecommunications Senior Officials' Meeting (TELSOM).

ATRC focuses largely on combating spam by sharing policies, strategies, and technical expertise. ATRC established the Working Group on Network Security in August 2004, originally called the Working Group on Anti-SPAM Strategies, to review measures by ATRC members to counter the emerging threat of spam. The theme fell in line with the Singapore Declaration's "Action Agenda" at the 3rd TELMIN in September 2003, and the name of the Working Group was subsequently changed at the 11th ATRC meeting in Malaysia in August 2005 after a Framework for Cooperation on Network Security and a corresponding Action Plan were adopted. [254] The Working Group's primary contribution has been a publicly accessible online Anti-Spam Database.[255]

TELSOM's mandate is to "identify, implement and monitor cooperation programs...; serve as a forum for exchange of information, discussion and consultation on major regional or international issues and developments in telecommunications...; promote participation of the private sector, regional/interregional organizations and non-governmental organizations...; and establish...working groups /expert groups." [256] TELSOM created the Working Group on ASEAN Information Infrastructure (WG-AII) with the following objectives:

- "To facilitate the establishment of the ASEAN Information Infrastructure by enhancing the design and standards of National Information Infrastructure (NII) of Member Countries and ensuring their interoperability and interconnectivity;
- To work towards establishing high-speed direct connection between the national information infrastructures with a view to evolving this interconnection into an ASEAN Information Infrastructure backbone;
- To work towards facilitating the setting up of national and regional Internet exchanges and Internet gateways, including regional caching and mirroring; and
- To promote the security and integrity of ASEAN Information Infrastructure." [257]

WG-AII's current activities include establishing a national Computer Emergency Response Team (CERT, see Chapter 5), establishing guidelines for information sharing among CERTs, developing a convergence policy framework, and compiling a National Information Infrastructure database. [258] In addition, WG-AII offers a publicly accessible online NII database, providing information on related topics by country or key indicator.[259] Since 2006, however, there do not appear to have been any updates to the ASEAN CONNECT websites for TELMIN and TELSOM.

4.2.3 Asia-Pacific Telecommunity (APT)

Established in 1979 by an initiative of the United Nations, the Asia-Pacific Telecommunity (APT) was formed to "...promote the explanation of telecommunication services and information infrastructure ... and facilitate coordination within the region with regard to major issues pertaining to telecommunication services." [260] APT has only started to play a role in the cyber security arena in the past few years, with an apparent focus on issues related to spam.

The APT organized a workshop on "CERT Best Practices" in Thailand in September 2004 in response to a request by participants at a seminar on Network Security Management and Positive Use of the Internet in Malaysia in August 2003. The workshop was attended by IT security experts, managers, and policy makers from member countries and regional and international organizations, and "provide[d] an opportunity for participants to understand the risks involved and strategies to protect their networks and databases from security threats." [261]

The APT held a subregional Meeting on Spam and Security, in collaboration with the Pacific Island Telecommunications Association (PITA), in October 2005, and a symposium in August 2005 on Network Security and Spam, at which "the objectives...were to promote the need for network security, increase the awareness of the harmful effects of spam, and promote regional and international cooperation on spam." [262] The APT held another symposium on Network Security at the 11th APT Standardization Program (ASTAP) Forum in Bangkok, Thailand, in June 2006.[263] However, only APT members have access to online symposium documentation.

The APT has included a link on its website to promote awareness of the need for network security and the problems associated with spam. The site "assists Members to explore the policy and regulatory issues associated with network security, and the regional initiatives and cooperation that are required to achieve secure networks." In March 2007, in an effort "to assist global cooperation in the fight about spam," the APT became an associate partner of the StopSpamAlliance (see Chapter 5). [264] The APT also gave a presentation on APT Spam Initiatives & Developments at the 12th ASTAP Forum in March 2007.[265]

The APT developed a strategic plan for 2006-2008, with a focus on developing sound ICT policy and regulatory frameworks, bridging the digital divide by fostering and facilitating ICT development, maximizing the benefits of APT programs through internal and external cooperation, and improving the efficiency and effectiveness of APT operations. Specifically related to cyber security, one of the APT's key areas of focus is ensuring network security and protection of privacy. The APT seeks to accomplish this by "facilitat[ing] development of national and regional strategies in the area of critical information and communications infrastructure protection, promot[ing] leveraging on public-private sector partnerships for the protection of these connected infrastructures, and promot[ing] intra-regional and inter-regional agreements on protection of privacy." [266]

4.2.4 United Nations Economic and Social Commission for Asia and the Pacific (ESCAP)

The United Nations Economic and Social Commission for Asia and the Pacific (ESCAP) is the "regional development arm of the United Nations for the Asia-Pacific region" and is the most comprehensive of the UN's five regional commissions. Established in 1947, ESCAP has its headquarters in Bangkok, Thailand, and represents sixty-two member governments, stretching from Turkey to Russia to New Zealand. ESCAP works primarily to overcome the region's greatest challenges, including poverty reduction, globalization management, and emerging social issues, by focusing on issues most effectively addressed through regional cooperation. [267] ESCAP's Information, Communication, and Space Technology Division (ICSTD), established in July 2002, is a "multi-disciplinary pool of experts dedicated to seeing the region benefit more thoroughly from ICSTstrengthened socio-economic development" by providing assessments on regional trends and an overview of emerging issues affecting its membership. [268]

In response to global developments in cyber security and emerging threats in the Asia-Pacific region, ESCAP has held frequent regional workshops related to public policy and information security for business development. At the Asia-Pacific Conference on Cybercrime and Information Security, held in Seoul, Korea, in November 2002, representatives from member nations met "to prepare a draft action plan on cybercrime and information security for submission to the regional preparatory meeting for [WSIS]" and to "promote cooperation to address cyber-crime and enhance information security in the Asia-Pacific region." [269] At the conclusion of the conference, working groups drafted a regional plan of action calling for increased stakeholder awareness and transfer of knowledge, improved policy, legal, and regulatory frameworks for promoting information security and addressing cybercrime, establishment of regional mechanisms to improve cyber security, increased protection against cybercrime, and improved detection of, and responses to, cybercrime.[270]

Since 2004, ESCAP has hosted numerous workshops, seminars, and symposiums on ICT capacity building and enabling policies and regulatory frameworks for ICT development in the Asia-Pacific region, many of which have included sessions on information security policy and standards. ESCAP also co-hosts annual meetings of the Regional Interagency Working Group on Information and Communication Technology (IWG), together with the ITU (see Chapter 3) and the APT (see above). At these meetings, held in Bangkok, Thailand, the IWG generally discussed issues related to follow-up on WSIS "with a major focus on the draft regional action plan towards the information society on Asia and Pacific." [271] In particular, the IWG made specific reference to WSIS Action Line C5 and the ITU's Global Cybersecurity Agenda (see Chapter 3) in the final report from the recent Eleventh IWG Meeting in February 2008.[272]

In recent years, ESCAP has also released major publications related to ICT policy. *Internet use for business development – an introductory set of training modules for policymakers* (2007) is "intended as an introductory guide to the various issues and legislative/policy options that developing countries should consider as they put into place the policies and rules that will encourage SMEs to take advantage of the Internet to create business opportunities." It includes an entire section on cybercrime and security for e-business and policymakers ("Module 3").[273] In addition, ICSTD's *Information Security for Economic and Social Development* (2008) deals with "key economic, legal, and social issues related to information security...[in order] to help countries get prepared to face issues and challenges linked to ICT deployment, uses, and misuses." [274]

4.2.5 China-Japan-Korea (CJK)

On October 7, 2003, the leaders of China, Japan, and Korea (CJK) held a summit meeting in Bali, Indonesia, where they issued a joint declaration on the "Promotion of Tripartite Cooperation among the People's Republic of China, Japan, and the Republic of Korea." At the first Three-Party Committee Meeting in China in June 2004, ministers agreed to submit an "Action Strategy on Trilateral Cooperation" (ASTC) for review at the next Trilateral Summit Meeting in November 2004. [275]

Since the Joint Declaration was made in 2003, CJK has formed several working groups focusing on "promoting harmonization and cooperation in ICT policy between the three parties." [276] These working groups originally focused on six areas: the next generation internet (IPv6), 3G and next generation mobile communications, network and information security, telecommunication service policies, digital TV and broadcasting, and open source software. [277] At the third Ministers' Meeting in Sapporo, Japan, in July 2004, the three parties agreed that "the rising demands in ICT fields called for a closer trilateral cooperation, and the framework of such cooperation was 'East Asia (CJK) ICT Summit.'" [278] In addition, a second next generation Internet (IPv6) Working Group meeting was planned for November 2004,[279] an "International Working Group" was established, and "Cooperation on RFID Sensor Network" was added to the CJK working group focus areas. [280]

With regard to cyber security, it was agreed at the third Ministers' Meeting that the East Asia (CJK) ICT Summit would include projects on network and information security policies and mechanisms, joint response to cyber attacks (including hacking and viruses), information exchange on online privacy protection information, and creation of a Working Group to promote this cooperation. [281] Nevertheless, a current status on this Working Group could not be found.

4.2.6 Asia-Pacific Incident Response

4.2.6.1 Asia Pacific Computer Emergency Response Team (APCERT)

Incident response coordination efforts in the Asia-Pacific rim are handled by the Asia Pacific Computer Emergency Response Team (APCERT). APCERT is a coalition of twenty teams from fourteen economies across the region and was formed in 2002.[282] The coalition's primary mission is CERT (see Chapter 5) information sharing and "...enhancing Asia Pacific regional and international cooperation on information security." [283] The 2005 Annual Report shows that APCERT has enabled regional cooperation. For example, the Australian government, through its Australian Agency for International Development (AusAID) program, has provided funding for in-country CSIRT training and held its annual Asia-Pacific IT Security Conference in May 2005.[284]

APCERT also holds Annual General Meetings to "provide an opportunity for APCERT members to meet, get to know each other, learn about issues affecting each other as CERTs, and most importantly, through shared goals and interests, to help each other and improve Internet security within each of [the] economies and throughout the Asia-Pacific region and beyond." [285] The February 2007 meeting focused on mobile malware, botnets, malware embedded websites, and social engineering.[286] The APCERT Annual Conference 2008 was recently held in Hong Kong, in March 2008, and included workshops on "Building a Distributed Intrusion Detection System using SurfIDS", "Advanced IT Audit & Control", and "In-Depth Network Security Monitoring (NSM) for Intrusion Analyst." [287]

In December 2006, APCERT organized an annual drill to "test the timeliness and response capability of leading CSIRTs (see Chapter 5) from Asia-Pacific economies. The drill focused on handling compromised web sites hosting malicious code designed for use in distributed denial of service (DDoS) attacks." [288] In November 2007, APCERT held another drill to test response capability in addressing regional cyber threats. The drill, which ranged across five time zones, simulated a cyber attack aimed at disrupting the Beijing 2008 Olympic Games and "focused on how to effectively minimize the impact of cyber attacks that primarily involve large scale malicious programs propagation and targeted attacks capable of impairing economic activity and which sought to affect political outcomes." [289] As an example of APCERT's regional influence, the Thai CERT indicated a much faster response to the Blaster virus in 2003, as compared to its response to the Slammer worm prior to cooperation with APCERT .[290]

APEC explicitly supports APCERT and recognizes the role of CSIRTs and the need to establish teams in member countries to promote information exchange and cooperation. To achieve this, APEC launched an initiative for a regional CSIRT in March 2003, aimed at providing in-country training to enhance capabilities in developing countries in the region and to develop guidelines.[291]

4.2.7 Asia-Pacific Law Enforcement Cooperation

In the Asia-Pacific region, law enforcement coordination and cooperation is primarily left to individual nations. As mentioned above, APEC's TEL has placed recent focus on cybercrime legislation and enforcement capacity building. There is no equivalent to Europol in the region and a majority of the efforts related to law enforcement occur through the APEC organization.

4.3 Americas

The primary regional intergovernmental organization responsible for promoting cyber security policy initiatives, regional cooperation, harmonization of domestic legislation, incident response, and law enforcement against cybercrime in the Americas is the Organization of American States (OAS), although other smaller organizations have also recently begun contributing to the global effort. An extensive survey of cyber security initiatives in Latin America has been documented in an ongoing study at the Georgia Institute of Technology, which can be accessed through the online Cyber Security Organization Catalog.

4.3.1 Organization of American States (OAS)

The Organization of American States (OAS) represents the largest regional cooperation effort within the Americas. Formed in 1948 by the Ministers of Justice or Ministers or Attorneys General of the Americas (REMJA), OAS is composed by thirty-five member states from the Western Hemisphere, and the organization is primarily concerned with interaction and cooperation among its member states. [292] Article 1 of the OAS Charter states that the goal of OAS member nations in creating the organization was "...to achieve an order of peace and justice, to promote their solidarity, to strengthen their collaboration, and to defend their sovereignty, their territorial integrity, and their independence." [293]

OAS is actively involved in furthering cyber security throughout the hemisphere. In June of 2004, the OAS's Committee on Hemispheric Security (part of the OAS Permanent Council) approved the adoption of a "Comprehensive Inter-American Strategy to Combat Threats to Cybersecurity: A Multidimensional Approach to Creating a Culture of Cybersecurity." This document is the guiding cybersecurity policy throughout the Americas, and was produced by the joint efforts of member states, their experts, and the technical expertise of OAS subgroups that will be detailed below, such as the Inter-American Committee Against Terrorism (CICTE), the Inter-American Telecommunication Commission (CITEL), and REMJA Group of Government Experts in Cybercrime. The main goals of this Strategy include establishing an integral, international and multi-disciplinary approach to creating a culture of cyber security in the hemisphere, promoting the creation of national CSIRTs, encouraging OAS member states to enhance international cooperation in cyber security matters, and supporting CICTE in the creation of an Inter-American Alert, Watch and Warning Network. [294]

Additionally, the OAS has also partnered with other regional and international organizations to host cyber security meetings and workshops, such as the December 2005 Conference on Cybercrime held in Madrid jointly by OAS and the Council of Europe. [295]

4.3.1.1 Inter-American Telecommunication Commission (CITEL)

The Inter-American Telecommunication Commission (CITEL) is an entity of the Organization of American States whose objective is to facilitate and promote the continuous development of telecommunications in the Hemisphere.[296] In its 2006 "Declaration of San Jose," representatives agreed "to promote the establishment of legal bases designed to strengthen confidence in and the confidentiality of communications, permit the ongoing growth of infrastructure, and combat the use of ICTs for criminal ends, thereby creating a culture of cybersecurity that ensues from the OAS cybersecurity strategy." [297]

CITEL has a working group specifically tasked with cyber security and critical infrastructure protection. The Rapporteur Group on Cybersecurity & Critical Infrastructure was created "to study the security aspects related to communication network development, its role in supporting other critical infrastructures, the role of the private sector in securing the communication network, and domestic and regional approaches required in the Americas Region on this matter." [298] Furthermore, the working group is tasked with "developing domestic and regional approaches to network security, deployment strategies, information exchange, and outreach to the public and the private sector; reviewing the various frameworks and guidelines on network and cyber security and their applicability within the Americas region; and fostering dialogue regarding the work of the ITU (i.e. Study Group 17) and other relevant fora on network and cyber security." [299]

In March of 1996, CITEL published the first edition of *Blue Book: Telecommunications Policies for the Americas*. Since then, the Blue Book has been updated twice, and the latest edition was published in 2005 in coordination with the ITU. The Blue Book is a "reference tool to provide the countries of the Americas Region with factual descriptions and information on telecommunication policy and regulatory issues, including the challenges and opportunities presented by the development of new telecommunication technologies." In particular, the Blue Book includes a section dedicated to Network Security and Critical Telecommunication Systems, which describes the OAS strategy for promoting cyber security and CIIP in the Americas through "...the establishment of an inter-American alert and watch network to disseminate cybersecurity information and to respond to crises, incidents, and threats to computer security,... the implementation of technical standards that facilitate the development of trustworthy and reliable information networks and systems, and... the adoption of national legal frameworks that protect information systems, prevent the use of computers to facilitate illicit activities, and punish cyber-crime." [300]

CITEL also holds regional workshops several times a year on combating fraud in telecommunication services, promoting information exchange, research, and discussion on legislation, regulation and control, technical and administrative tools, and inter-State and inter-sectorial mutual cooperation mechanisms to minimize the effects of fraud. These include the First and Second Workshops on the Impacts of Fraud on the Provision of Telecommunications Services for Users,

States, and Operators in 2007, and several workshops to be held in 2008 pertaining to fraud in telecommunication services, world telecommunication standardization, and association between member states in the Americas to achieve better telecommunication development in the region. [301]

4.3.2 Latin American Cooperation of Advanced Networks (CLARA)

The Latin American Cooperation of Advanced Networks (CLARA) is a non-profit, regional intergovernmental organization created in November of 2004 to provide connectivity to the Americas and link national research and education networks within Latin America and with other networks in Europe (GEANT2), the United States (Internet2), Asia (APAN) and the rest of the world. RedCLARA represents the interests of many Latin American nations including Argentina, Bolivia, Brazil, Colombia, Costa Rica, Cuba, Chile, Ecuador, El Salvador, Guatemala, Honduras, Mexico, Nicaragua, Panama, Paraguay, Peru, Uruguay, and Venezuela. The organization's objectives are "to establish the coordination between the National Academic Networks of Latin America and with other blocks; to foster the cooperation for the promotion of the scientific and technological development; to plan and implant networks services for the regional interconnection; and to develop a regional network (RedCLARA) to interconnect to the national academic and research networks." [302]   Since its creation, RedCLARA has established a platform that links 12 countries and 729 universities throughout the Americas at speeds of up to 622Mbps. [303]

4.3.2.1 CLARA Security Task Force (GT-Seg)

In April 2005, CLARA created a Security Task Force (GT-Seg) based on CSIRTs participation (see Chapter 5) to "promote a security culture in the Latin American and Caribbean region." The initial objective for GT-Seg was to implement CSIRT capabilities in each Member State and to promote collaboration among those created. Today, GT-Seg is also committed to establishing computer security frameworks in each member state, promoting the development of new CSIRTs in the region, providing a discussion forum for information sharing, facilitating exchange and data correlation of security incidents, promoting a coordinated response to security incidents, disseminating security best practices for academic environments, building an updated database of security points-of-contact for each member state, and cooperating with other regional initiatives. [304]

GT-Seg is also referred to as GT-CSIRT on the CLARA website. More information on the role of GT-CSIRT can be found in the section below on Americas Incident Response.

4.3.3 Americas Incident Response

4.3.3.1 Inter-American Committee Against Terrorism (CICTE)

The OAS Inter-American Committee Against Terrorism (CICTE) addresses cyber security through work on incident response in the Americas region. In particular, CICTE's objective vis-à-vis cyber security is to "strengthen the Member States' capacity to comply effectively with the requirements of the OAS Comprehensive Inter-American Strategy to Combat Threats to Cyber Security..., support the establishment of national CSIRTs (see Chapter 5) and the creation of a hemispheric network of CSIRTs..., [and] coordinate activities with the OAS working group on cybercrime of the Ministers of Justice (REMJA) and the Inter-American Telecommunication Commission (CITEL, see above)." CICTE provides technical assistance to member states to help them implement their national CSIRTs, provide training to designated CSIRT personnel, and establish a network of CSIRTs in the region. [305]

CICTE holds frequent meetings, workshops, and conferences on cyber security throughout the Americas that emphasize CIIP, cyber terrorism, and incident response. In July 2003, CICTE hosted its first Conference on Cyber Security in Buenos Aires, Argentina. Further meetings were held in Ottawa, Canada (March 2004), Sao Paolo, Brazil (September 2005), and in San Jose, Costa Rica (April 2007). [306] Additionally, in the past two years CICTE has hosted several cyber security training courses for the creation and management of CSIRTs, including those in Brasilia, Brazil (June 2007), Antigua, Guatemala (April 2008), and Bogota, Colombia (May 2008).[307] According to CICTE, twelve countries in the Western Hemisphere have established CSIRTs thus far.[308] However, despite recent progress with CSIRT development throughout the region, the project to create an Inter-American CSIRT Watch and Warning Network, which first emerged in 2004, is still only in the planning stages today.[309]

In April 2006, CICTE held its first Cyber Security and Cyber Crime Workshop in Miami, Florida, followed by a second in November 2007. [310] The purpose of these workshops was "to cover segments at the policy and technical levels, and to increase collaboration and strategic partnerships between participating OAS Member States and private corporations and Academia to better protect critical infrastructures from the cyber threat." [311]

CICTE has also approved several declarations pertaining to cyber security. In March 2007, CICTE approved the "Declaration of Panama on the Protection of Critical Infrastructure in the Hemisphere in the Face of Terrorism," which reaffirmed OAS' commitment to earlier resolutions on cyber security, including the "Comprehensive Inter-American Cybersecurity Strategy," the 2003 "Declaration on Security in the Americas," and the 2006 "Declaration of San Carlos on Hemispheric Cooperation for Comprehensive Action to Fight Terrorism" which aimed at developing secure communication technologies and recognized CICTE's work in promoting CIIP in the Americas. [312]

4.3.3.2 CLARA Computer Security Incident Response Team (GT-CSIRT)

The role of the CLARA Computer Security Incident Response Team (GT-CSIRT) is to promote incident response initiatives in the Americas similar to those of TF-CSIRT and APCERT in Europe and Asia-Pacific, respectively. Although GT-CSIRT appears more targeted at the incident response activities of the CLARA Security Task Force (GT-Seg), no difference between the two groups can be easily determined from the CLARA website. The GT-Seg Action Plan for 2006-2007 included proposals for defining security profile roles for each Member State, requesting directive support to define security contacts, promoting the establishment of new CSIRTs in the region using a Security Training and Education Program (STEP), building a security best practices digital repository, organizing regular meetings and seminars as part of the Security Awareness Program (SAP), collaborating with other CLARA Task Forces and Working Groups, and promoting collaborative activities among regional and international CSIRTs. [313]

GT-CSIRT has also worked on translating material from TERENA and FIRST (see Chapter 5) for training use in Latin America, as well as organizing three workshops in Central and South America between September and November 2006 "to promote and teach how to create, operate, and establish a CSIRT and security community" in all CLARA Member States. In addition, a 2006 Security Awareness CD would be delivered to all Member States to disseminate information on CSIRT teams, security basics, and security for all users (including beginners). Although no metrics or other information could be found on the success of these objectives (or whether or not they actually occurred), the group has also proposed follow-up work, as well as distribution of a 2006-2007 Survey, calling for further participation from members, implementing security forums, creating security videos from basic security (Podcast), Wiki, RSS news, etc. [314]

4.3.4 Americas Law Enforcement Cooperation

Similar to the Asia-Pacific region, law enforcement coordination and cooperation in the Americas region is left primarily to individual nations. There is no equivalent to Europol, nor does the OAS participate substantially in efforts specifically related to cybercrime law enforcement. The OAS Group of Government Experts on Cyber-Crime, however, has recently concentrate on the development and harmonization of cybercrime legislation, as described below, including procedural measures for investigation and prosecution.

4.3.4.1 Group of Governmental Experts on Cyber-Crime

The OAS Group of Governmental Experts on Cyber-Crime has a mandate to perform the following actions: complete a diagnosis of criminal activity that targets computers and information or that uses computers as the means of committing an offense; complete a diagnosis of national legislation, policies, and practices regarding such activity; identify national and international entities with relevant expertise; and identify mechanisms of cooperation within the Inter-American system to combat cybercrime.[315]

During the Fourth Meeting of the Group of Governmental Experts on Cyber-Crime in February 2006, the Group identified several recommendations in order to comply with the mandate discussed above and enhance cooperation amongst the members. Specifically, the Group instructed members to identify the authorities that are to serve as points of contact for international cooperation in the area of cybercrime. These points of contact will be compiled and maintained in a directory by the OAS. Additionally, the Group ascertained training programs are necessary regarding the G8 24/7 Network of Contacts for High-Tech Crime (see Chapter 3), as well as in cybercrime and management of electronic evidence. It also encouraged members to compile the "cybercrime laws of the OAS member states, including their substantive and procedural aspects as well as the area of mutual legal assistance, and make this information available to the OAS member states on the Internet webpage, so that that information may be used, among other purposes, for training in the area." Members are also instructed to develop an "inventory of the most common forms and means of cyber-crime in the member states, disseminate it through the private 'Internet' page, and present it to the group of experts at its next meeting for consideration." [316] In response to directives from the Fourth Meeting, three OAS Regional Technical Workshops were held during 2006 and 2007 to provide training in the areas of electronic evidence management and the 24/7 Network of Contacts for High-Tech Crime.[317]

The Fifth Meeting of the Group of Governmental Experts on Cyber-Crime, which occurred in November 2007, addressed issues such as developments on the OAS cyber security strategy, cooperation between the private sector and government authorities, and the Council of Europe Convention on Cybercrime, which no Latin American country has yet ratified – although Mexico and Costa Rica have recently been invited to access.[318] [319] In response to these issues, members recommended that states assign units for the investigation and prosecution of cybercrime, identify points of contact for international cooperation, adopt legislation to criminalize cybercrime and collect electronic evidence, immediately join the G8 24/7 Network of Contacts for High-Tech Crime, implement measures from the Council of Europe's Convention on Cybercrime, strengthen information exchange and international cooperation, and develop partnerships with law enforcement and the private sector. In addition, the OAS Secretariat General was encouraged to update the online Inter-American Cooperation Portal on Cyber-Crime and continue to document cybercrime laws from member states. Finally, the Group expressed satisfaction with the results obtained from the three workshops described above, and accepted an offer by the U.S. government to help train OAS member states in developing cybercrime legislation and procedural measures for investigation and prosecution. [320]

In addition to recent meetings and workshops related to cybercrime, the OAS Group of Governmental Experts on Cyber-Crime also offers Online Training and Technical Guides, including a "Best Practices for Computer Forensics" manual, several questionnaires on cybercrime for member states, a listing of national cybercrime legislation initiatives to date, and links to other international and regional organizations combating computer crime. [321]

5 Private-Public and Non-Governmental Organizations (NGOs)

As a majority of the world's network infrastructure is shared and managed by both public and private entities, organizations in both sectors are dependent on each other for the stability and security of ICTs and critical infrastructure. While private industry is often a step ahead of the government in security research and development, governments are responsible for constructing, adopting, and enforcing the laws and policies that frame the environment in which private industry performs. Given that the ownership and operation of a significant portion of the world's network infrastructure is managed by private organizations, governments must work in tandem with these organizations to ensure the ongoing success of their work.

A wide range of partnerships exists today among public and private organizations with ICT security objectives. Such arrangements are made for the accomplishment of specific objectives in the context of a particular sector or a particular type of attack. Due to independent initiatives and uncoordinated actions by many of these organizations, the amount of progress has been somewhat difficult to measure and evaluate.

5.1 Advocacy Groups

5.1.1 Anti-Spam

5.1.1.1 Coalition Against Unsolicited Commercial Email (CAUCE)

The Coalition Against Unsolicited Commercial Email (CAUCE) is a consumer advocacy group of volunteers, originally formed to encourage the creation of anti-spam legislation. Today, its goal has expanded to "defending the interests of the average Internet user." [322] CAUCE US, the original organization, merged with its Canadian counterpart, CAUCE Canada, in March 2007 to become CAUCE NA and, after the merging of CAUBE.AU (Australia) and CAUCE India into APCAUCE (Asia-Pacific), an international CAUCE was finally created in 2002, called iCAUCE.[323] By distributing information and organizing member meetings, the CAUCE groups attempt to raise public awareness on spam-related issues by "actively advocat[ing] on behalf of consumers to governments, legislators, law enforcement agencies, and industry associations about matters related to the blended threat of spam, viruses and spyware." In addition, the main CAUCE website contains helpful links and postings on news and current events related to the global fight against spam.[324]

5.1.1.2 London Action Plan (LAP)

The London Action Plan is an international effort of government and public agencies from twenty-seven countries to improve cooperation in spam law enforcement. Drafted in October 2004, the plan involves the combined efforts of OECD, the ITU, EU, APEC, and many other organizations. Under the plan's framework, all participants are encouraged to do their utmost in their respective areas of expertise and with their individual resources. Additionally, each participant is to coordinate its efforts with other agencies having the proper authority to regulate spam within its country and designate a point of contact from its organization in order to facilitate efficient communication between groups. In periodic communications, such as quarterly conference calls, participants exchange and discuss information, including new developments and trends, new data, effective enforcement strategies, organizational initiatives, and training sessions. They are also directed to seek cooperation with external sources and, furthermore, are to encourage and support the involvement of less developed countries and organizations in the effort to regulate spam.[325]

London Action Plan members and their counterparts with the European Union Contact Network of Spam Authorities (CNSA, see Chapter 4) periodically hold joint workshops. In November 2005, members organized a workshop in London focused on the use of spam databases, gathering data for spam trends, investigative assistance and complaints referral, and regional case studies and enforcement actions.[326] A third workshop was recently held in October 2007 in Washington D.C., and included training sessions for law enforcement agencies, sessions on public-private cooperation initiatives, and sessions on cross-border enforcement cooperation.[327] LAP members are also planning an upcoming joint conference with CNSA and ENISA (see Chapter 4) in Wiesbaden, Germany, in October 2008, which will focus on law enforcement training and "spam scams." [328]

5.1.1.3 Messaging Anti-Abuse Working Group (MAAWG)

The Messaging Anti-Abuse Working Group's (MAAWG) stated purpose is "to bring the messaging industry together to work collaboratively and successfully address forms of messaging abuse such as messaging spam, virus attacks, and denial-of-service attacks." To resolve the messaging abuse problem, MAAWG has focused on targeting three key initiatives: collaboration, technology, and public policy. In order to collaborate as an industry to jointly combat abuse, MAAWG hopes to "develop an ISP code of conduct, develop a trusted inter-carrier network for messaging, [and] develop and share industry best practices among organizations." In exploring architectural frameworks and technology options to best combat abuse, MAAWG hopes to "define a reference architecture and network standards for combating messaging abuse, including reduction of spoofing and preventing of identity forgery." Finally, to address issues related to public policy, MAAWG hopes to "effectively engage with policy makers" by "building effective interfaces to key standards and legislative bodies." [329]

Rather than viewing messaging as "just email," the organization desires a more holistic approach, one that should include new types of messaging and draw support from members across industries and across the globe.[330] As such, its impressive 122-member roster (fifteen sponsor members, sixteen full members, and ninety-one supporting members) includes major telecommunications companies of various sizes and specializations.[331] To facilitate improved communication and cooperation among its member organizations, MAAWG launched the MAAWG Abuse Contact Database, a database of email contacts that provides members with direct access to appropriate contacts at other MAAWG companies to assist in resolving various issues, such as reputation, malware, and fraud.[332] Member organizations also convene twice a year in addition to the annual General Meeting, which is open to both member and non-member organizations.[333] The proceedings are made available on MAAWG's website, along with various other whitepapers, metrics, and publications.

In October 2007, MAAWG was issued the "first best practices developed cooperatively by major Internet and email service providers for managing infected subscribers." The organization proposed using "walled gardens," closed online environments created by services providers, which act as safe areas to which infected users may be automatically redirected when attempting to access the Internet. After disinfecting their systems in a walled garden, the users are again granted web access. By using walled gardens in this manner, MAAWG hopes to inhibit the spread of botnets across the Internet. [334]

MAAWG joined the StopSpamAlliance in June 2007 and the London Action Plan (LAP, see Chapter 3) in February 2008, advancing its global cooperation against online abuse. In addition, the group recently addressed social networking threats at a meeting in March 2008 and offered email authentication best practices to help industry reduce spam in April 2008. [335] In June 2008, MAAWG is planning its 13th General Meeting in Heidelberg, Germany, and its 14th General Meeting is currently planned for September 2008 in Fort Lauderdale, Florida, United States. [336]

5.1.1.4 Spamhaus Project

Spamhaus, founded in 1998 and now based in Geneva, Switzerland, and London, United Kingdom, is a non-profit organization dedicated to tracking Internet spam gangs and the mitigation of spam effects using real-time, spam-blocking databases made available to both administrators and general users. In addition, Spamhaus is a participant in several international efforts against spam, including the London Action Plan (LAP, see Chapter 3).[337]

A dedicated team of twenty-five investigators and forensics specialists from around the world manage the organization, which has created three major "block lists" (DNSBLs) available to the public. The Spamhaus Block List (SBL) consists of the IP addresses of verified spam sources and is updated to reflect the emergence of new issues and the resolution of existing issues twenty-four hours a day, seven days a week.[338] A special subset of this list, known as the Don't Route Or Peer (DROP) list, is "an advisory 'drop all traffic' list...of stolen 'zombie' netblocks... controlled entirely by professional spammers."[339] The Exploits Block List (XBL) contains the IP addresses of illegal third party exploits, incorporating data from two trustworthy DNSBL sources.[340] Finally, the Policy Block List (PBL) stores a set of "end-user IP address ranges which should not be delivering unauthenticated SMTP email to any Internet mail server except those provided for specifically by an ISP for that customer's use."[341] Recently, the three DNSBLs have been combined into a single, comprehensive block list, dubbed "ZEN."[342]

In addition to block lists, Spamhaus also maintains a database of "[collated] information and evidence on known spam operations that have been terminated by a minimum of three ISPs for spam offenses" (known as ROKSO, the Register of Known Spam Operations). Spamhaus made available to law enforcement agencies a special version of ROKSO that contains records with evidence, logs, and information on illegal activities. According to the organization, 80% of spam is generated by only two hundred such spam operations.[343]

5.1.1.5 StopSpamAlliance (SSA)

The StopSpamAlliance is a cooperative international effort organized by APEC, CNSA, the ITU, LAP, OECD, and the Seoul-Melbourne Anti-Spam group. In 2007, the effort was joined by APT, the Messaging Anti-Abuse Working Group (MAAWG, see below), the Internet Society (ISOC, see below), the Asia Pacific Coalition Against Unsolicited Commercial Email (APCAUCE), and CAUCE North America. The objective of the StopSpamAlliance is to help coordinate international action against spam and related threats more effectively by gathering information and resources to improve information sharing among participating entities.[344]

"In line with the WSIS Tunis Agenda, which asked members to 'deal effectively with the significant and growing problem posed by spam' and called upon
all stakeholders to adopt a multi-pronged approach to counter spam, the Stop-
SpamAlliance pages link to initiatives in the field of anti-spam legislation and enforcement activities, consumer and business education, best practices, and international cooperation." [345]

The StopSpamAlliance serves primarily as a central event and information
notification mechanism for member organizations and visitors, as its website is
filled with current news on upcoming conferences, summits, and meetings regarding cyber security and spam. While its individual members have ongoing projects
and successful accomplishments, however, the alliance itself does not appear to
have undertaken any unified initiatives as a group. [346]

5.1.1.6 The European Spambox Project (SPOTSPAM)

The European Spambox Project (SPOTSPAM), derived in September 2005
from the European Commission's *Safer Internet Programme* (EU, see Chapter 4),
was a twenty-four month contracted pilot project intended "to facilitate legal action against spammers at the international level" [347] by drawing up "self-regulatory
strategies which can help protect end users against spam." [348] Through a comprehensive network of national Spamboxes, spam complaints were stored in a central
SPOTSPAM database and directed to the appropriate authorities, including plaintiff ISPs, plaintiff companies, and public authorities. Legal action was then facilitated by "making available information stored in the database based on strict
rules." [349]

Over the course of the project's twenty-four month lifetime, members from
SPOTSPAM worked together with other organizations, such as Microsoft, eco,
and The Research and Academic Computer Network (NASK) to discuss and collaborate on project goals and strategies. In November 2005, SPOTSPAM was
presented at the Spam Enforcement Conference in London, hosted by the Department of Trade and Industry (DTI) and CNSA (see Chapter 4), as well as a separate
meeting between SPOTSPAM, FTC Spambox, and Industry Canada. In early
2006, the project was presented again to CNSA at a workshop in Brussels, and to
Messagelabs and Spamhaus (see above), interested in how individual countries
could "support or regulate the development of the database scheme." In a March
2006 meeting with the French database project SignalSpam, project leaders agreed
to share technical developments and strive to make their projects work comple-
mentary. Finally, in September 2006, the final SPOTSPAM pilot database and
spambox implementation was presented at the fourth German Anti-Spam Summit
in Cologne, Germany. [350]

In the SPOTSPAM Project Final Report, released on the eco website in May 2007, it was reported that the prototype database and national Spambox were successfully implemented, the operations manual and agreements between actors were completed, and that SPOTSPAM was expected to go live in the coming days. [351] No information on the outcome of the project, however, could be found.

5.1.2 Anti-Phishing

5.1.2.1 Anti-Phishing Working Group (APWG)

The Anti-Phishing Working Group (APWG) is a volunteer "global pan-industrial and law enforcement association focused on eliminating the fraud and identity theft that results from phishing, pharming, and email spoofing of all types." With over three thousand public and private members, including over seventeen thousand companies and agencies worldwide, nine of the top ten U.S. banks, and the top five U.S. ISPs, the APWG is the largest known organization dedicated to the global fight against phishing. Aside from offering a number of resources to its members, including monthly trend reports, a repository on known phishing attacks, a collection of best practices, future threat models and forensics, and a variety of guides and white papers, the APWG's most significant impact has been its participation in and presentations to ongoing regional and international conferences throughout the year. [352]

In 2007, for example, speakers from APWG presented at the Hack.lu security conference in Luxembourg, the OAS II Cyber Security and Cyber Crime Workshop in Miami, Florida, USA, the Council of Europe's conference on identity theft and cybercrime in Tomar, Portugal, and a UNODC meeting on identity-related crime in Courmayeur, Italy. In 2008, APWG conducted a presentation for the Ministry of Economy, Trade, and Industry (METI) in Tokyo, Japan, the APCERT Annual General Meeting in Hong Kong, the Council of Europe's OCTOPUS Interface Conference on Cooperation Against Cybercrime in Strasbourg, France, the Federal Trade Commission (FTC), the SoftForum's CODEGATE Hacking & Security Conference in Seoul, Korea, the World Cyber Security Summit in Kuala Lumpur, Malaysia, and the Financial Services Technology Consortium's (FSTC) Annual Conference in California. [353]

The APWG is also hosting its own Counter-eCrime Operations Summit (CeCOS II) in May 2008 in Tokyo, Japan. The summit will "engage questions of operational challenges and the development of common resources for the first responders and forensic professionals who protect consumers and enterprises from the eCrime threat every day." [354] The eCrime Researchers Summit will be held in

October 2008 in Atlanta, Georgia, USA, in conjunction with the 2008 APWG General Meeting and will "bring together academic researchers, security practitioners, and law enforcement to discuss all aspects of electronic crime and ways to combat it." [355]

5.1.3 Anti-Spyware

5.1.3.1 Anti-Spyware Coalition (ASC)

The Anti-Spyware Coalition (ASC) is "dedicated to building a consensus about definitions and best practices in the debate surrounding spyware and other potentially unwanted technologies. Composed of anti-spyware software companies, academics, and consumer groups, the ASC seeks to bring together a diverse array of perspectives on the problem of controlling spyware and other potentially unwanted technologies." [356] The ASC, whose members include a variety of different types of organizations, from NGOs to multinational companies, such as Google, is primarily an advocacy group for organizations against spyware. In promoting public awareness and education, the ASC provides numerous anti-spam resources on its website, including tips documents for consumers and corporations, a conflicts resolution document, a best practices suggestions document, definitions and supporting documents, a risk model description, and considerations for anti-spyware product testing. [357]

One of the Coalition's primary endeavors is to inform members of the general public on how to protect themselves from spyware, often through numerous publications available on its website and occasional public workshops. At its first public workshop "Defining the Problem, Developing Solutions," in Washington, D.C., in February 2006, participants focused on the impact of spyware on businesses and individuals, an overview of solutions, education, policy and enforcement, corporate security, and industry guidelines.[358] Since then, the ASC has held subsequent workshops on "International and Cross-Border Solutions" (Ontario, 2006) and "Spyware: What's Worked, What's Left, and What's Coming" (Washington, D.C., 2008). In addition, the ASC has participated in panels at the Black Hat and Defcon conferences in August 2007 in Las Vegas, Nevada, USA. [359]

5.1.4 Anti-Botnets

5.1.4.1 International Botnet Task Force (BTF)

The International Botnet Taskforce (BTF) is a "worldwide coalition of public and private sector computer security specialists" [360] who "share best practices, tools, and training to combat botnets and ultimately to assist law enforcement in prosecuting [bot-herders]." [361] Microsoft, responsible for development of this organization, hosted its first meeting in October 2004 in order to provide training for international law enforcement officials, such as INTERPOL (see Chapter 3), confronting the task of investigating botnet abuses. [362] By June 2007, the initial group of fifteen participating national law enforcement agencies had rapidly grown to thirty-five, along with fifty technology industry participants. [363]

Aside from its training regimen, the organization joined with the FBI and Carnegie Mellon University to carry out Operation Bot Roast, an ongoing initiative to thwart bot-herders and disrupt and dismantle their botnets in June 2007. [364] Ongoing investigations have since identified over one million victims, and the FBI has already begun prosecuting several herders, while simultaneously providing information to the owners of the infected machines. [365] In November 2007, the FBI, again with the assistance of the Carnegie Mellon CERT/CC and the International Botnet Task Force, indicted another eight individuals responsible for more than $20 million in economic loss and more than one million victim computers in Operation Bot Roast II. According to Robert S. Mueller, the current FBI Director, "…In Bot Roast II, we see the diverse and complex nature of crimes that are being committed through the use of botnets… and will continue to be aggressive in finding those responsible for attempting to exploit unknowing Internet users." [366]

Because the International Botnet Task Force does not have a known website, information on recent initiatives and annual conferences is extremely difficult to track. The 5th International Botnet Task Force Conference appears to have been held in Redmond, Washington, in January 2007, although no further information could be found regarding its outcome. [367] In addition, the group appears to have held another recent conference in February 2008 in Lyon, France. [368]

5.2 Incident Response

5.2.1 Computer Security Incident Response Teams (CSIRTs)

A Computer Security Incident Response Team (CSIRT), or Computer Emergency Response Team (CERT), is a group of trained security experts that investigate security breaches, evaluate cyber defenses, and analyze the state of information security within its corresponding area of jurisdiction. The Computer Emergency Response Team/Coordination Center (CERT/CC) at Carnegie Mellon University was the first CERT, created by the Software Engineering Institute under U.S. federal mandate in response to the Morris worm in 1988.[369] Today, there are numerous CERTs and CSIRTs worldwide, working both independently and in collaboration to address cyber security incidents and promote awareness. Security experts from the Carnegie Mellon University Software Engineering Institute have released *Incident Security Teams for Developing Countries* to highlight recent progress of emerging incident security teams responding to cyberization in developing countries around the world.[370]

5.2.2 Forum of Incident Response and Security Teams (FIRST)

The most significant global alliance of CSIRTs is the Forum of Incident Response and Security Teams (FIRST), an international confederation of 195 CSIRT teams from forty-three countries that have combined resources to share information and promote incident prevention in the international ICT community.[371] The organization promotes international cooperation by hosting conferences for nonmembers, encouraging the development of CSIRTs, and sharing technical information, tools, methodologies, and best practices. Although FIRST is a truly international effort to address cyber security, its membership is exclusive, which limits countries with less developed capabilities from joining its ranks.[372]

FIRST maintains an extensive library of guides and publications based on material submitted by organization members, designed to assist both members and the general public in configuring systems securely according to configuration templates and security guidelines.[373] More information on FIRST can be found in the Carnegie Mellon University Software Engineering Institute's *Incident Security Teams for Developing Countries.* [374]

5.3 Policy, Education, & Public Awareness

5.3.1 Authentication and Online Trust Alliance (AOTA)

The Authentication and Online Trust Alliance (AOTA) is a non-profit corporation founded in 2004 by business, marketing, and industry leaders, including Microsoft and Symantec, originally seeking to promote solutions to and improve user confidence in authenticated email. Following successful turnout at three national summits between 2004 and 2007, the organization later expanded its scope to online trust and confidence in the broader sense. The organization's mission today is "to create a trusted ecosystem and to foster the elimination of email and Internet fraud, abuse, and data intrusions, thereby enhancing online trust, confidence, and online protection of businesses and consumers" through facilitation of best practices, data sharing, implementation of online trust solutions, and promotion of online safety worldwide. [375]

In addition to the organization's role in facilitating annual summits on online trust and authentication issues, AOTA functions through the work of numerous working committees and chairs, each focusing on a different target area, such as authentication, brand/domain protection, education and events, privacy and data governance, and public policy and governmental affairs. In particular, the Technical Committee works to "identify, evaluate, and advocate technological solutions to fight email and Internet fraud, abuse, and data intrusions." [376] AOTA also offers a variety of informative resources on its website, dealing with online trust and confidence, including summit presentations and additional information on technical standards, such as DomainKeys Identified Mail (DKIM) and Sender ID Framework (SIDF), as well as non-technical resources, such as the 2008 Business and Industry Resource Directory and 2008 Authentication Compliance Reports, including Fortune 500 companies and FDIC member banks. [377]

In January 2008, AOTA issued several calls to action to industry leaders and online retailers, including an initial attempt to form an Online Trust Ecosystem to combat Internet abuse, in which industry leaders would commit to online safety, security, and privacy. [378] AOTA also issued a call to action for industry adoption of Extended Validation Secure Sockets Layer (EV SSL) Certificates- "an emerging standard to help verify site identity and increase consumer confidence in eCommerce and banking," [379] reiterating on its website its affirmation to "stand behind EV certificates and promot[e] adoption as a key tool to help the entire online trust ecosystem." [380]

AOTA also released an Authentication Press Release and Call to Action for Brand and ISP Authentication Compliance in January 2008, encouraging Fortune

500 and industry retailers to adopt DKIM and SIDF- the current standards for domain and email authentication- to protect consumers from spam and phishing attacks.[381] Results on the corresponding study on industry compliance were published in the report "State of Email Authentication and the Internet Trust Ecosystem," available for download from the AOTA website.[382]

At the most recent AOTA Summit 2008: *Reaching the Tipping Point: Future of Online Trust*, held from June 4-5 in Seattle, Washington, industry representatives from leading organizations such as Microsoft, PayPal, and VeriSign participated in plenary discussions on a variety of issues pertaining to online trust and cyber security, such as emerging threats, trust in email, blogs, social networks, and online banking, best practices with ISPs and Registrars, computer espionage, data leakage and governance, an implementation guide to email authentication, business value from EV SSL Certificates and DKIM/SIDF, browser security, and insights from participating IT and Marketing Executives.[383] Immediately following the Summit, the AOTA Email Deliverability & Trust Academy provided an educational opportunity for attendees to gain invaluable "insights and practical application guidance from leading marketers, ISPs, and deliverability consultants." [384]

5.3.2 Global Information Infrastructure Commission (GIIC)

The Global Information Infrastructure Commission (GIIC) is an organization devoted to the realization of a sustainable, equitable information society that "enhances the economic and social well-being of people everywhere" and defines itself as a "confederation of chief executives and other officers of business firms engaged in the development, manufacture, deployment, operation, modernization, financing, and use of services and products based upon information and communication technologies." Largely a policy oriented body, it "[advocates] the promulgation, adoption, and enforcement of responsive public policies, [seeks to] convene forums to address policy challenges, [desires collaboration] with other sectors of society, conducts formal studies," and shares the results of its efforts. [385]

GIIC recognizes information security as an important component in the pursuit of its goals. Thus, in collaboration with the Business and Industry Advisory Committee to the OECD (see Chapter 3), the International Chamber of Commerce (ICC), the International Telecommunications Users Group (INTUG), and the World Information Technology Services Alliance (WITSA) – together labeled the Alliance for Global Business (AGB) – the organization drafted the *Global Action Plan for Electronic Business*, updated in July 2002. This document addressed the future of electronic business and associated policies, providing a framework in which policymaking for electronic commerce should take place as well as an argument to the involvement of governments, private corporations, and other organizations. [386]

The *Global Action Plan* specifically addressed the issues of identity management and end-user security. In particular, it encouraged businesses to continue the development of security technologies for electronic commerce, called for government support of private sector research and development in the field of security technology, advocated consumer choice in cryptographic systems that suit the needs of each individual case, requested the removal of export controls on cryptographic technologies, and advocated discussion of legal interception of telecommunications by both government and business. There were also a number of items advocating self-regulation by business in the field of digital signatures, smart cards, and other technologies associated with electronic commerce. [387] Although GIIC continues to actively promote global ICT-based initiatives today, no record of any subsequent work on cyber security research could be found since 2002.

5.3.3 International Chamber of Commerce (ICC)

The International Chamber of Commerce (ICC) is an organization of businesses throughout the world that believes in the global economy as "a force for economic growth, job creation, and prosperity." [388] The ICC advocates the positions of its members and is often a policy making body in such areas as anti-corruption, banking techniques and practices, e-business, and ICTs. With regard to cyber security, the ICC's Commission on E-Business, IT, and Telecoms (EBITT) includes the Task Force on Security and Authentication, which has the following objectives:

- "Improve network and information security in businesses and for other users by raising awareness and providing practical tools to assist in making security a higher priority for all users;
- "Ensure legislation and policy related to information security, electronic signatures and authentication is properly informed with the necessary information to understand evolving and relevant technologies, business processes and business needs, and support increased use of these technologies." [389]

To achieve these objectives, the ICC provides several resources online for businesses to use in promoting secure ICTs. In an early attempt to address issues related to Internet security, the ICC released in 1997 its *General Usage for International Digitally Ensured Commerce* (GUIDEC), followed by an updated version (GUIDEC II) in October 2003, "to establish a general framework for the authentication of digital messages, based upon existing law and practice in different legal systems." [390] In March 2003, in response to growing member concerns about the Council of Europe Convention on Cybercrime (see Chapter 2), the former ICC Task Force on Cybercrime/Cyber Security issued a set of recommendations to signatory states when implementing the Convention and its Additional Protocol within a business context. [391]

In November 2003, the ICC released *Information Security Assurance for Executives*, in conjunction with the OECD Business and Industry Advisory Committee (OECD, see Chapter 3), as "part of the effort of international business to create a truly global 'culture of security,'" based on principles of awareness, responsibility, response, ethics and democracy, risk assessment, security design and implementation, security management, and reassessment.[392] The ICC also issued a policy statement on spam in December 2004, identifying key terminology, principles, and recommendations for members in combating unsolicited commercial electronic messages.[393] Most recently, in June 2006, the ICC prepared a *Framework for consultation and drafting of information compliance obligations*, highlighting information compliance problems posing major obstacles for business, as well as principles for constructive legislative practices for information compliance.[394]

5.3.4 International Federation for Information Processing (IFIP)

The International Federation for Information Processing (IFIP) is a nongovernmental, non-profit umbrella organization devoted to ICT and science, representing ICT societies from fifty-six countries and regions. The organization provides for the exchange of ideas, information, and experience by sponsoring more than one hundred conferences annually, and is divided into fourteen Technical Committees.[395]

Technical Committee Eleven (TC11), the Security and Protection in Information Systems Committee, specifically seeks to "increase the reliability and general confidence in information processing as well as to act as a forum for security managers and others professionally active in the field of information processing security." To achieve this aim, TC11 seeks to engage in "the establishment of a common frame of reference for information security, the exchange of practical experience in security work, the dissemination of information on and the evaluation of current and future protective techniques, and the promotion of security and protection as essential elements of information processing systems." [396]

In order to accomplish its objectives, TC11 has established a number of working groups. Each is devoted to a specific area of interest in security, including security management, small systems security, data and application security, network security, identity management, information technology misuse, information security education, digital forensics, critical infrastructure protection, and trust management. In addition, each group has its own organizational structure and objectives, and is responsible for hosting a number of independent conferences and workshops, and making available relevant articles and publications. [397]

IFIP's 23rd International Information Security Conference (IFIP SEC 2008) will convene as part of the IFIP World Computer Congress (WCC) 2008 in Milan, Italy, in September 2008. IFIP WCC 2008 will provide a forum for the exchange of knowledge, ideas, and experience among worldwide experts in ICT fields.[398] In March 2007, IFIP Working Group 11.10 hosted the *1st Annual WG 11.10 International Conference on Critical Infrastructure Protection* at Dartmouth College, New Hampshire, where it facilitated discussions on infrastructure vulnerabilities, security challenges, sector interdependencies, case studies, legal, ethical, economic, and policy issues related to critical infrastructure protection, SCADA security, and telecommunications network security.[399] At IFIP SEC 2007 in Sandton, South Africa, IFIP presented on new approaches for security, privacy, and trust in complex environments, including topics such as applications of cryptography, new approaches to fraud management systems, information security culture, digital forensics, information warfare, intrusion detection, privacy enhancing technologies, trust models and management, and information security metrics.[400]

5.3.5 Open Information Systems Security Group (OISSG)

The Open Information Systems Security Group (OISSG) is an independent, non-profit organization seeking to "spread information security awareness [by creating] an environment where security enthusiasts from [around the world can] share and build knowledge." [401] Membership is open to any enthusiast who shares the organization's vision and is willing to conform to its ethical requirements. Currently, OISSG consists of a diverse group of individuals in forty-two local chapters worldwide, including five in the United States.[402] The local chapters organize conferences, workshops, and both formal and informal meetings, as well as provide a medium for personal interaction, general information, exchange of ideas, and collaborative work on any of the organization's various projects that were initially conceived during these meetings.[403]

OISSG conducts research in several security fields. Its vulnerability research team reverse engineers code and discretely informs the affected software vendors of exploitable flaws under its disclosure policy.[404] [405] The password security research team documents existing authentication systems and related tools, releases password guidelines, and develops new means of authentication.[406] The disaster recovery team is tasked with the evaluation of business continuity and disaster recovery plans as well as formulation of new strategies and the means to test them.[407] The organization also has teams developing threat metrics and a Java vulnerability scanning framework for databases.[408] [409] In addition, OISSG offers a library of links on its website to popular tools, articles, and websites related to information security.[410]

By far the largest ongoing project OISSG has undertaken is the Information Systems Security Assessment Framework (ISSAF), described as "an effort to develop an end-to-end framework for security assessment" and an attempt to "provide a single point of reference for professionals involved in security assessment."

[411] A constantly evolving framework, the ISSAF is designed to serve as a comprehensive source of information that integrates a number of existing management tools and internal controls. In this way, the framework provides guidance in identifying an organization's vulnerabilities and evaluating its existing security policies and practices.[412] Associated ISSAF "sister projects" include the following:

- The Computer Crime Investigation Framework (CCIF), which serves as an informative tool regarding cybercrime for law enforcement.[413]
- The Security Essentials Framework (SEF), which covers the fundamentals of information security for those who are new to the field.[414]
- Capture the Flag (CTF), which involves a series of challenges in defeating information security measures on a target system.[415]

OISSG also holds worldwide conferences and presentations "to raise the level of information security awareness and to teach advanced security practices developed by OISSG." The most recent conference was the "FIST-Conference Delhi: Hack and Investigate," held in Delhi, India, in May 2004. Previous conferences included "Routing and Routing Protocol Security" in Jaipur, India, in March 2004, "Web Application Security" in Frankfurt, Germany, and "Network Security" in Madrid, Spain, in February 2004, "DNS Security," "File systems Security and Integrity," and "Properties and Security of the 802.11b Wireless Networks" in Madrid, Spain, in November 2003. [416]

5.3.6 Society for the Policing of Cyberspace (POLCYB)

The Society for the Policing of Cyberspace (POLCYB, or "Cyber-Pol") is a non-profit organization founded in 1999 in British Columbia, Canada. The society's goal is "to enhance international partnerships among public and private professionals to prevent and combat crimes in cyberspace." The Society works to promote information sharing, public education on information protection and Internet safety, and public awareness on cybercrime through Quarterly and Annual General Meetings, international conferences, and public education forums. [417] In addition, the Cyber-Pol website includes numerous links and other resources related to cybercrime and information security awareness.

Through partnerships with investigators, senior and executive managers in criminal justice, law enforcement officials, forensic accountants, trainers for criminal justice and corporate agencies, judiciary and practitioners in legal professions, academics, and policy analysts, Cyber-Pol also works "to provide corporate victims with the police contacts to investigate and apprehend the attackers while allowing corporations to control dissemination of their sensitive information." In particular, the Society focuses its work on current and emerging issues in cyber security, such as economic crime, computer hacking, biometrics, cyber-terrorism, Internet child pornography, and telecommunications fraud. [418]

POLCYB held its last Quarterly Meeting in March 2008 on "Unlawful Access to Information: Perspectives on Prevention, Detection, and Response," and included speakers from Walt Disney Co. and Sun Microsystems Inc., as well several representatives from local and regional law enforcement agencies.[419] At the Society's last Annual General Meeting, held in December 2007, participants discussed "Strengthening the Industry/Government Partnership Globally" and included a keynote presentation from the Data Protection Officer and CISO of Motorola, Inc.[420]

Cyber-Pol is also widely recognized for its well-represented international cybercrime conferences and summits, such as the recent Annual Policing Cyberspace International Summit on "International Policing and Policy Perspectives on Countering Cybercrime," including Post-Summit Digital Evidence Training. The Summit was held in November 2007 in collaboration with the Council of Europe (see Chapter 4) in Bangkok, Thailand, and included presentations on topics such as digital forensics, current international cybercrime trends and threats, data protection, privacy and identity management, e-Money laundering in financial sectors, child exploitation, building "trusted communities" in the Virtual World, and pharmaceutical crime on the Internet. [421] [422] The next POLCYB International Summit is currently scheduled for November 2008 in Bangkok, Thailand, and will focus on the theme "Towards the Future of Global Cybersecurity: Raising the Bar on Collaboration." [423] In addition, the next POLCYB Policing Cyberspace International Conference is currently planned for September 2008 in Vancouver, Canada, on the theme "International Research and Collaboration in Cybersecurity," including a keynote presentation on "Dark Web Terrorism Research." [424]

5.3.7 SysAdmin, Audit, Network, Security (SANS) Institute

The SANS (SysAdmin, Audit, Network, Security) Institute was established in 1989 as a center for cooperative information security research and education. Today, SANS claims to be "the most trusted and... the largest source for information security training and certification in the world" and reaches more than 165,000 security professionals around the world. SANS maintains a wealth of knowledge and resources on nearly all aspects of information security and manages the Internet Storm Center – the "Internet's early warning system." [425]

SANS offers a variety of training courses in general information security, security auditing, security management, legal issues related to computer security, and secure application development. Many of these courses involve hands-on experience with the latest advances in security technology, such as security in Oracle, Linux, and .NET, computer forensics, network penetration testing, intrusion detection, wireless security, web application security, VoIP security, network worm and bot analysis, malware detection, security policy, CIP, ethics in ICT, and software security awareness. Courses are offered around the world throughout the year in locations such as Australia, Finland, Canada, Switzerland, Japan, Egypt, and United Arab Emirates. [426] Together with the Global Information Assurance Certification (GIAC), SANS also offers opportunities and events at which students can earn GIAC Security Expert (GSE) and GSE-Malware certifications, including the Network Security 2008 Conference in Las Vegas, Nevada. [427]

In December 2007, SANS hosted a Cyber Defense Initiative in Washington, DC, offering various courses on hacker techniques, exploits, and incident handling; forensics, investigation, and response; and web application security.[428] SANSFIRE 2008, which also took place in Washington, DC, featured a specialized course on Critical Infrastructure Protection (CIP) with a distinct focus on the "scope of critical infrastructure vulnerabilities, the dependence of critical infrastructures on the Internet, and Internet security problems." [429] In October 2008, SANS will host a Summit Series on WhatWorks in Forensics and Incident Response in Las Vegas, Nevada, inviting anyone to attend from the public and private sectors to learn more about advanced threats and effective techniques for protecting information systems.[430]

SANS also develops, maintains, and publishes an abundance of free information security resources for public access, including an Information Security Reading Room which contains over 1600 computer security white papers in over seventy categories; high-level security newsletters; and an up-to-date knowledge base on the current top twenty most critical Internet security vulnerabilities. In addition, SANS offers security webcasts, including one in September 2008 on the top seven trends in incident response and computer forensics, as well as a SANS portal for members to create customized security webpages. General Internet users also have access to a variety of frequently asked questions on topics such as malware and intrusion detection, as well as a glossary of security terms. [431]

The SANS Internet Storm Center (ISC), established in 2001 following discovery of the Li0n worm, "provides free analysis and warning service to thousands of Internet users and organizations, and is actively working with Internet Service Providers to fight back against the most malicious attackers." The ISC consists of a core, all-volunteer team of security experts and intrusion detection analysts who gather millions of intrusion detection logs from around the world to identify and alert the Internet community to emerging threats and attacks in cyberspace. The ISC issues general reports on its findings, including severity of attacks, attack metrics, and background on the underlying computer vulnerabilities or exploits. In an effort to promote information sharing, "all Internet users are welcome to use the information in the... reports and database summaries to protect their network from intrusion attempts." [432]

The SANS Software Security Institute (SSI) "provides training, certification and a library of research and community initiatives to help developers, architects, programmers, and application security managers protect their software/web applications." SSI offers numerous training and certification opportunities on topics such as web application security and hacking, language specific secure coding, software security testing, and Payment Card Industry (PCI) compliance. [433] In May 2008, SANS SSI announced its first European partnership for secure programming education with K.U. Leuven DistriNet in Leuven, Belgium. The goal of the partnership was "to enhance the security curriculum of students..., to exchange teaching practices..., and to provide easy access for European companies to SANS-SSI knowledge and certification." [434]

Aside from general cyber security research, training, and education, SANS also supports the global initiative to secure cyberspace in other ways. For example, in May 2008, SANS announced at the International Multilateral Partnership Against Cyber-Terrorism (IMPACT) World Cyber Security Summit in Kuala Lumpur, Malaysia, that the Institute would commit $1 million for a Joint Cyber Defence Program to expand the cyber security capacity of developing countries. The improved program would focus on "train[ing] teachers to deliver intense, hands-on courses in key cybersecurity skills like forensics, intrusion detection, penetration testing, and more so that regardless of income levels every country can provide world-class training to its cyber defenders." [435]

5.3.8 World Information Technology and Services Alliance (WITSA)

The World Information Technology and Services Alliance (WITSA), founded in 1978, is a "consortium of over sixty information technology industry associations from economies around the world," representing over ninety percent of the global ICT market. WITSA is an advocacy group, identifying itself as "the global voice of the IT industry," and is dedicated to promoting the growth and development of the industry through appropriate public policy, international trade and investment, the sharing of knowledge and experience, the exchange of information, and the creation of a "forum for identifying common issues and views." [436] [437] With particular relevance to cyber security, WITSA has a Task Force on Electronic Commerce and a Task Force on Critical Information Infrastructure. [438]

WITSA is known for two flagship events, held once every two years in different nations. The Global Public Policy Conference (GPPC), held most recently in Cairo, Egypt, in November 2007, generally focuses on global policies affecting the ICT industry, including those related to information security and cyber-crime. [439] Conference speakers at Plenary Session VI presented on personal data protection and digital identity management, consumer protection and empowerment, holistic approaches to network and information systems security, alignment of incentives for stakeholders to increase security, ensuring "privacy by design," cross-border law enforcement for online privacy and security, ensuring satisfactory Internet requirements for CIIP, and balancing law enforcement needs with freedom, privacy, and business impacts. [440] The next GPPC conference will be hosted in Bermuda in 2009. [441]

The World Congress on Information and Technology (WCIT), held last in May 2008 in Kuala Lumpur, Malaysia, is a "global ICT forum that brings together global leaders in business, government and academia," and is often billed as the "Olympics of ICT." [442] Speakers representing public and private interests from around the world gathered at the 2008 Congress to discuss current ICT challenges, opportunities, and perspectives, including a debate on cyber security and a final presentation by Dr. Vinton Cerf, Vice President & Chief Internet Evangelist for Google, on "Tracking the Internet into the 21st Century." [443]

For the past ten years, WITSA has been extremely active in releasing public statements on issues related to information security, cybercrime, CIIP, and law enforcement. In 1998, the Alliance released an early statement on "Government and Law Enforcement Access to Transmitted Information in the Digital Environment," indentifying several principles to address business concerns related to confidentiality, legal access, encryption, and personal privacy.[444] In 1999, the Alliance released a statement on "Critical Information Protection (CIP): A Framework for Government/Industry Dialogue," which focused on industry responsibilities for building and operating critical information infrastructures, globalization, communication, and coordination of CIP activities, legal frameworks, and education.[445]

In February 2000, WITSA released results of a study, based on a survey of thirty-nine countries' ICT associations, concluding that "cyber security would be the next 'top priority' issue facing the I[C]T industry around the globe." [446] In collaboration with McConnell International, the Alliance further prepared a report in December 2000 on "Cyber Crime… and Punishment? Archaic Laws Threaten Global Information," finding that, after analyzing the state of the law regarding cybercrime in fifty-two countries, "only ten of these nations have amended their laws to cover more than half of the kinds of crime that need to be addressed," recommending that:

- "Firms should secure their networked information.
- Governments should assure that their laws apply to cyber crimes, and
- Firms, government, and civil society should work cooperatively to strengthen legal frameworks for cyber security." [447]

In May 2000, WITSA issued a statement to the G8 Heads of Delegations expressing concerns about an early draft of the Council of Europe's Convention on Cybercrime, claiming the proposed draft was contrary to one of the Alliance's principles on transmission of information.[448] In a November 30, 2000, press release, WITSA further expressed its concerns, claiming that "often the most effective way to counter cybercrime is through technical innovation, not burdensome legislation." However, despite announcing support for the Convention's objectives of promoting international law enforcement cooperation and mutual legal assistance "to address criminal law and procedural aspects of various types of offending behavior directed against computer systems," [449] the Alliance continued its debate on legality of the Convention on Cybercrime. In 2004, it released a "Background Paper on Traffic Data Requirements and Cooperation with Law Enforcement Authorities," providing recommendations for government and industry on promoting law enforcement using data preservation, rather than data retention, collection techniques.[450]

WITSA also releases frequent publications on its own research and initiatives, as well as those of other ICT-related organizations around the world. The organization's online white papers, presentations, critiques, and newsletters are generally available to both members and the general public. In May 2006, WITSA released its "Information Security: Building a Sustainable Program" association toolkit "to assist ICT associations in building a robust information security program to promote policies that benefit the ICT sector in their countries." The toolkit includes Information Security Program Development and Advocacy Work Plan templates, as well as an overview of WITSA priorities and recommendations for implementing national cyber security strategies. [451] WITSA also recently published on its website results of an eGovernment Survey in Athens, Greece, in October 2006, to document current challenges and barriers to eGovernment initiatives, such as security issues, in WITSA member countries. [452]

WITSA recently participated in the 2007 Internet Governance Forum in Rio de Janeiro, Brazil, at which it presented several recommendations for guiding the development of global information security policy. Based on earlier statements on information security released in May 2002[453] and June 2005[454], WITSA communicated at the 2007 IGF its focus and principles on joint government-industry cooperation, international government cooperation on critical information infrastructure programs, industry incentives for work on cyber security research, development, and training programs, adoption of industry information security standards and best practices, and preservation of communication data for law enforcement purposes. [455]

5.3.8.1 Global Internet Project (GIP)

The Global Internet Project (GIP) Advisory Committee to WITSA is an independent, non-partisan, "international group of senior executives committed to fostering continued growth of the Internet," representing members from Internet-centric industries throughout Asia, Europe, and North America. In an effort to promote industry action to minimize government regulation of ICTs, the GIP encourages governments and industry to achieve solutions to Internet policy challenges through the distribution of publications, hosting workshops and conferences, and consulting decision-makers around the world. [456]

The GIP contains numerous online resources on information security, including original publications, information on initiatives and events, and links to documents from other notable organizations and companies. In particular, the GIP has contributed original work on several publications and presentations related to infrastructure protection/cyber war, security and reliability of NGN, and promoting a global culture of cyber security through government-industry cooperation; the most recent publications, however, are from 2003. [457]

5.4 Research, Development, & Standardization

5.4.1 3rd Generation Partnership Project (3GPP)

The 3rd Generation Partnership Project (3GPP) is a collaboration of international telecommunications standards bodies created in 1998 "to produce globally applicable Technical Specifications and Technical Reports for a 3rd Generation Mobile System based on evolved GSM core networks and the radio access technologies that they support," including the maintenance and development of the Global System for Mobile communication (GSM) Technical Specifications and Technical Reports.[458] The primary 3GPP technical body responsible for GSM Security is the Technical Specification Group on Services and System Aspects – Working Group 3 (TSG SA WG3, or S3).

In addition to its responsibility for the security of 3GPP, TSG SA WG3 also "perform[s] analyses of potential security threats to the system, consider[s] the new threats introduced by the IP based services and systems, and set[s] the security requirements for the overall 3GPP system." In addition, SA WG3 "continuously analyze[s] the security implications of new services being developed." [459] Through the collaboration of its Organizational Partners (including ETSI, see Chapter 4), in 2002 3GPP developed the first specifications for 3GPP Confidentiality and Integrity Algorithms, as well as early GSM Security Algorithms.[460]

TSG SA WG3 maintains a comprehensive website listing of technical 3GPP security specifications,[461] documentation from various international meetings and conferences,[462] and an up-to-date listing of active 3GPP work items specific to SA WG3. Active 3GPP work items include studies on lawful interception, consumer protection against spam and malware, enhanced security architecture and enhancements, and visibility and configurability of security in 3GPP systems.[463]

TSG SA WG3 has also hosted a wealth of working group meetings in various countries around the world since 1999. These meetings allow Organizational Partners and international liaisons to discuss such topics in 3GPP security research as lawful interception, network domain security, algorithm requirements, and access security. [464]

5.4.2 Central and Eastern European Networking Association (CEENet)

The Central and Eastern European Networking Association (CEENet), created in 1994, is a non-profit partnership of over twenty national research and education networks working "to coordinate the international aspects of the academic, research, and education networks in Central and Eastern Europe and in adjacent countries." CEENet's work is typically accomplished through conferences, workshops, and courses in network technology, publications, promotion of national network services, exchange of technical information to research networks, and formation of working parties to undertake relevant technical activities. [465]

Network security and security training and awareness have been common themes at CEENet workshops and conferences, including a presentation on Security and Accessibility at the Second CEENet Workshop on Network Management, co-hosted with NATO, in Ohrid, Macedonia, in June 2000[466] and a presentation in March 2005 on "Training and Funding for Security Related Projects" at the AZ-Net Conference in Baku, Azerbaijan.[467]

5.4.3 Cooperative Association for Internet Data Analysis (CAIDA)

The Cooperative Association for Internet Data Analysis (CAIDA) is a collaboration of private and public organizations working to "provide the world with a neutral framework to support cooperative technical endeavors that have the potential to be critical in meeting the demands of an exponentially growing system of networks." Created in 1997 at the San Diego Supercomputing Center (SDSC) in San Diego, California, CAIDA was founded on the principles of collaboration and cooperation and seeks to promote research on global ICT-based challenges and develop useful tools and strategies for Internet Service Providers and other relevant stakeholders within the industry. [468]

CAIDA works to promote advances in security research through the collaborative work of its members on malicious network and infrastructure activity research and analysis, storage of security data for researchers, and dissemination of security publications to members, partners, and other relevant stakeholders within the industry. By focusing on network-based attacks, data hosting and provision, and measurement and statistical analysis of the impact of cyber attacks on the global network infrastructure, CAIDA aims "to develop meaningful and up-to-date quantitative characterizations of attack activity and to produce fundamental insights into the nature of malicious behavior on the Internet and consequently the best directions for mitigating that behavior." Between 2001 and 2006, CAIDA released several analytical reports on some of the most widespread, malicious threats identified at the time, including the Nyxem Email Virus (2006), the Witty Worm (2003), and Code-Red (2001). [469]

In recent years, CAIDA has participated in many international venues to present research and findings on emerging security threats, such as a discussion on Blackworm at the Internet Security Operations and Intelligence (ISOI) II Workshop at Microsoft Headquarters in Redmond, Washington, in January 2007. [470] CAIDA also presented findings on current network security threats at TERENA Networking Conference 2007 [471] and, most recently, released a survey report with the American Registry for Internet Numbers (ARIN) in May 2008 on regional IPv6 penetration. [472]

5.4.4 GSM Association (GSMA)

In recent years, the widespread use of wireless devices, such as cellular phones and handheld computers, for mobile voice and web communications has become a critical infrastructure on which many businesses, governments, and individuals have become especially dependent for fast, reliable portable network communications. Unfortunately, due to rapidly changing standards and communication protocols used around the world, global initiatives to secure mobile applications and wireless communication networks have lagged far behind those oriented towards hardwired networks and traditional computing systems.

The GSM Association (GSMA) represents over eighty-six percent of the world's mobile phone connections and works "to ensure mobile phones and wireless services work globally and are easily accessible, enhancing their value to individual customers and national economies, while creating new business opportunities for operators and their suppliers." [473]

GSMA has an extensive mobile fraud and security program, including research and development on mobile application security (MAS) and GSM security algorithms. In February 2005, GSMA's MAS Project Team published a final summary of findings on GSM security, providing background, deliverables, and recommendations for improvement, concluding that "the identified barriers to prevent malware need to be further validated and strengthened," and recommendations would need to be realized through operator individual activities. [474] In addition to working with industry leaders to mitigate the identified barriers, GSMA has also begun work on an Open Mobile Terminal Platform (OMTP) project. [475]

GSMA has also developed several mobile security algorithms used "to provide authentication and radio link privacy to users on a GSM network," including the 3GPP Confidentiality and Integrity Algorithms (UEA2 and UIA2), as well as the 3GPP A5/3 and GEA3 Algorithms. All developed GSMA algorithms are available to qualified industry parties, including GSM network operators and manufacturers of eligible GSM equipment. [476] GSMA also manages the Security Accreditation Scheme (SAS), a voluntary audit program for GSM suppliers to validate the comprehensive security of their production sites and processes, benefiting both suppliers and network operators.[477]

The GSMA Certified Fraud Training programme was launched in May 2005 "to give the most up-to-date skills and knowledge to those whose job it is to detect fraudulent activity and to minimize its financial impact on an operator's business." [478] With organized training modules on identifying fraud, profiling fraud, analyzing fraud, and fraud and risk management, the training program was designed "so that measurable learning outcomes can be established and a progression in competence achieved by students as they move forward through the whole programme." [479] GSMA offers numerous training sessions throughout the year in Droitwich, England, hosted by fraud management experts from Focus Group Ltd.[480]

In addition to development, certification, and training initiatives, GSMA also offers individual mobile phone users helpful security advice on their website. In particular, the webpage serves as a knowledge bank for users on critical issues such as safe and secure use of GSM phones, preventing mobile phone theft, spam and mobile phones, computer viruses and mobile phones, and secure use of voicemail services, in addition to offering a complete FAQ on GSM itself. [481]

5.4.5 Institute of Electrical and Electronics Engineers (IEEE)

The Institute of Electrical and Electronics Engineers (IEEE) is a non-profit organization created in 1963 to "advance the theory and application of electro-technology and allied sciences; serve as a catalyst for technological innovation; and support the needs of its members through a wide variety of programs and services." [482] Today, with more than 375,000 members from more than 160 countries around the world, IEEE claims to have become "the world's leading professional organization for the advancement of technology." [483]

The IEEE Computer Society's Technical Committee on Security and Privacy (TCSP) hosts many workshops and conferences on ICT security and privacy, including most notably the IEEE Symposium on Security and Privacy and the Computer Security Foundations (CSF) Symposium. The IEEE Symposium on Security and Privacy, hosted in cooperation with the International Association for Cryptologic Research (IACR), is claimed to be "the premier forum for the presentation of developments in computer security and electronic privacy, and for bringing together researchers and practitioners in the field." [484] The 2008 Security and Privacy Symposium was held in Oakland, California, in May 2008 and included workshops on Digital Forensics and Web 2.0 Security and Privacy.[485] The 30th IEEE Symposium on Security and Privacy will be held again in Oakland in May 2009,[486]

The TCSP CSF Symposium is also held annually "for researchers in computer security to examine current theories of security, the formal models that provide a context for those theories, and techniques for verifying security." CSF Symposiums are typically informal and open, are held at various locations around Europe and North America, and consist of paper presentations and discussion panels. The most recent CSF Symposium (CSF-21) was held in Pittsburgh, Pennsylvania, in June 2008 and was collocated with the 23rd IEEE Symposium on Logic in Computer Science at Carnegie Mellon University. [487] CSF-21 included workshops on Automated Reasoning for Security Protocol Analysis, Security and Rewriting Techniques, Proof-Carrying Code, Formal and Computational Cryptography, and Analysis of Security APIs.[488]

In addition to annual workshops and conferences, IEEE Computer Society publishes a periodical called *IEEE Security & Privacy*. This periodical focuses on security issues of the day, such as wireless security, enterprise security, infrastructure security, digital rights management, cybercrime, and security education. The primary objective of the magazine is "to stimulate and track advances in information assurance and security and present these advances in a form that can be useful to a broad cross-section of the professional community-ranging from academic researchers to industry practitioners." [489] TCSP also releases a newsletter called *Cipher*, which contains Committee book reviews and conference reports, as well as news briefs related to advances in information security around the globe.[490]

5.4.6 International Organization for Standardization (ISO)

The International Organization for Standardization (ISO) is a non-governmental organization and network of national standards institutes from 157 countries. Headquartered in Geneva, Switzerland, it "forms a bridge between the public and private sectors" to develop and publish the world's largest repository of International Standards.[491] Often working in collaboration with ITU-T Study Group 17 (see Chapter 3) and the International Electrotechnical Commission (IEC), ISO has developed and published several international standards on cyber security, including *ISO/IEC 7064:2003* and *ISO/IEC 9796-2:2002*,[492] and frequently references the ITU-T Security Standards Roadmap in developing international security standards.[493]

Much of ISO's work on cyber security is accomplished through technical committee ISO/IEC JTC1/SC 27 ("IT security techniques"), which focuses on standardization of generic methods and techniques for IT security, including the following components:

- "Identification of generic requirements...for IT system security services,
- Development of security techniques and mechanisms,

- Development of security guidelines (e.g. interpretative documents, risk analysis), and
- Development of management support documentation and standards (e.g. terminology and security evaluation criteria)." [494]

In the ISO/IEC JTC1/SC 27 business plan for 2007-2008, the Committee indicated an expansion and refocus of its work, approaching new areas such as biometrics, identity management, and privacy. At the time the business plan was released, the Committee cited fifty-two active projects and sixty-two publications, as well as new projects on information security management systems auditing, verification of cryptographic protocols, ICT readiness for business continuity, guidelines for cyber security, and guidelines for application security. ISO/IEC JTC/SC 27 Working Groups most recently held meetings in 2006-2007 in South Africa, Russia, and Switzerland, and the most recent SC 27 Plenary meetings were held in May 2007 in St. Petersburg, Russia, and April 2008 in Kyoto, Japan. The Committee also co-hosted recent workshops with ITU-T in late 2007 on Cyber Security and Identity Management Standards. [495]

In addition to the work of ISO/IEC JTC1/SC 27, the ISO/IEC/ITU-T Strategic Advisory Group on Security (SAG-S) was created in January 2004 by the ISO Technical Management Board (TMB) to "conduct a review of existing ISO deliverables related to information security, ...assess the needs of all relevant stakeholders, ... assess relevant [security] standards developed by other organizations, ...recommend actions to be taken by the ISO Council, [and] submit a final report to the ISO/TMB and ISO Council..." In response, SAG-S developed a three-dimensional security model – focusing on targets, threats, and countermeasures – to identify "potential needs for security standards, existing standards, and gaps." In the group's 2005 final report, SAG-S emphasized that "security is a matter of urgent global concern" and provided recommendations to ISO for implementing security guidelines for technical committees, launching a security standards web portal, preparing an International Workshop Agreement on Emergency Preparedness, and drafting a Security Management System Framework standard. [496]

At the 5th Meeting of the ISO/IEC/ITU-T Strategic Advisory Group on Security in Geneva, Switzerland, in January 2008, the chairman of SAG-S suggested developing a "road map" of security standards, ensuring continuation of security workshops, and establishing an "annual report." Several reports were presented on continuing Subgroup initiatives, progress on the ISO Security Web Portal, publication of *ISO/PAS 22399* in 2007, and ongoing ITU-T and IEC security-related development and standardization projects. Presentations were also made on *ISO/IEC 27001* and recent workshops were held on Transit and Water Security. [497]

5.4.7 Internet Engineering Task Force (IETF)

The Internet Engineering Taskforce (IETF) is organized by its parent organization, the Internet Society, and is a "large open international community of network designers, operators, vendors, and researchers" concerned with the evolution of the Internet architecture and its smooth operation.[498] Its mission is "to produce high quality, relevant technical and engineering documents that influence the way people design, use, and manage the Internet" in order to improve its functionality.[499] Specifically, the organization identifies and proposes solutions to operational and technical problems, specifies the development of protocols and architecture in order to solve such problems, makes recommendations for the standardization and usage of Internet protocols, and provides a forum for information exchange.[500] To this end, the IETF elicits the input and expertise of its members, who are employed in various corporate, academic, and private organizations across the globe. The IETF has declared itself "open to any interested individual."[501]

The IETF accomplishes its technical work in the form of various working groups, a number of which are devoted to Internet security. In particular, the "IETF Security Area" provides links to ongoing security topics within the group, including a current proposal on "Key Management for Routing and Transport Area Protocols."[502] Members of each working group collaborate via mailing lists, and groups typically make any documentation of their findings available online, both for review by other IETF members and for the general public. The organization also conducts meetings three times per year.[503]

5.4.8 Internet Research Task Force (IRTF)

The Internet Research Task Force (IRTF), supported by ISOC (see below) and the IETF (see above), was created "to promote research of importance to the evolution of the future Internet by creating focused, long-term and small Research Groups working on topics related to Internet protocols, applications, architecture and technology." The IRTF Chair is appointed by the Internet Architecture Board (IAB), which serves a dual purpose as both an IETF committee and an advisory body to ISOC. In addition, each IRTF Research Group Chair is selected in consultation with the Internet Research Steering Group (IRSG), which manages the Research Groups and holds occasional workshops on both general and specific research priorities important to the evolution of the Internet.[504] The IRTF Research Groups most actively engaged in security are the Anti-Spam Research Group (ASRG), the Crypto Forum Research Group (CFRG), the IP Mobility Optimizations (Mob Opts) Research Group, and the Peer-to-Peer Research Group (P2P RG),

Focusing on technology solutions and standardization efforts within the IETF, ASRG "investigates tools and techniques to mitigate the effects of spam" and last presented its findings at IETF 60 in San Diego, California, in 2004.[505] CFRG "provides a forum where cryptographers, network security experts, and protocol designers can exchange ideas and investigate ways for using new cryptographic developments in the future Internet," although the group's website has not been updated with any activity since its inception in 2002.[506]

The Mob Opts Research Group accomplished several milestones between 2006-2007, including development of two IP Mobility testbeds and research on Mobile IPv6 Optimizations Enhancements Taxonomy and Location Privacy Solutions, as well as Multi-access Mobility and Session Key Management.[507] P2P RG, which "offers a forum for researchers to explore a broad range of fundamental P2P issues," provides, among other things, research on security of P2P systems, including "reputation-based trust for ad-hoc systems, or more centralized, CA [Certificate Authority]-like approaches." [508] No indication of progress on research specific to security, however, could be found on the group's website.

5.4.9 Internet Society (ISOC)

The Internet Society (ISOC) is a "non-profit organization founded in 1992 to provide leadership in Internet-related standards, education, and policy. With offices in Washington, DC, and Geneva, Switzerland, it is dedicated to ensuring the open development, evolution and use of the Internet for the benefit of people throughout the world." [509] Acting as a "global clearing house for Internet security information and education," ISOC works to promote a secure Internet infrastructure by "facilitating discussions on key policy decisions and initiatives towards self-government of the Internet through debate and development of position papers, white papers, and statements on Internet security related issues." [510] In late 2007, ISOC expanded its focus and abilities for 2008-2010 from its three traditional "pillars" of Standards, Public Policy, and Education, to longer-term, more strategic activities in the areas of Enabling Access, InterNetWorks, and Trust & Identity- all of which include some relation to cyber security.[511]

ISOC's most notable information security event is the annual Network and Distributed System Security Symposium (NDSS), held in San Diego, California, in February of each year, bringing together a large group of security researchers, implementers, and experts to "learn about and discuss cutting-edge advances in the science and application of network and distributed systems security." [512] [513] Due to the ever-increasing number of security issues and topics of discussion, the most recent NDSS conferences were extended to an unprecedented three full days.[514] ISOC also organizes annual INET Conferences to bring users, technologists, and policymakers together from around the world to host formal Internet-related discussions and workshops. Originally an annual global event, INET conferences have evolved into more targeted regional events, typically held alongside other conferences or meetings. [515]

The ISOC-EMEA (Europe, Middle East, and Africa) Security Expert Initiative (SEINIT), completed in 2006, was a two-year contract sponsored by the European Commission "to address the areas of security and privacy within the context of the IPv6 protocol." At the end of the two years, the SEINIT project had successfully developed a trusted, dependable, inter-operable, and ubiquitous security framework for next generation Internet infrastructures. [516] In addition, the ISOC Board of Trustees met in early October 2007 to facilitate open discussion on the subject of trust within the context of network enabled relationships, including themes of security, privacy, protection of personal data, assurance, and management of threats. [517]

ISOC has also recently been involved in a number of activities to promote awareness and dialogue on combating spam. In addition to offering a "Spam Policy Primer" on its website, describing the organization's key anti-spam objectives, ISOC provides links to informative publications on current spam initiatives in the global community. The ISOC chaired the ITU Telecom World 2006 Spam Workshop in Hong Kong, at which it encouraged policymakers "to address spam through coordination of the various measures that leverage one another," including technical solutions, education and awareness building, international cooperation, and public-private partnerships in establishing regulatory measures. [518]

5.4.10 Organization for the Advancement of Structured Information Standards (OASIS)

The Organization for the Advancement of Structured Information Standards (OASIS) is a non-profit consortium founded in 1993 consisting of over 5000 vendors and users from one hundred countries and representing over six hundred organizations committed to the "development, convergence, and adoption of open standards for the information society." In particular, OASIS hosts two online information portals on XML and web services standards, Cover Pages and XML.org, both widely regarded by the online open security standards community.[519] In addition, OASIS co-sponsors educational conferences and seminars, interoperability demonstrations, webinars, and industry events "that promote the importance and status of open standards." [520]

Through the work of twelve security-oriented technical committees, OASIS works to develop "security standards needed in e-business and Web services applications... [to] define foundational as well as application-level specifications." The OASIS technical committees on eXtensible Access Control Markup Language (XACML), Provisioning Services, Security Services, and Web Services Secure Exchange (WS-SX) have specifically been approved as standards by the

OASIS membership at large in recent years.[521] Other OASIS technical committees working on ongoing research and development of innovative ICT security standards include the Biometric Identity Assurance Services (BIAS) Integration Technical Committee, the Cross-Enterprise Security and Privacy Authorization (XSPA) Technical Committee, the Digital Signature Services eXtended (DSS-X) Technical Committee, the Enterprise Key Management Infrastructure (EKMI) Technical Committee, the Open Reputation Management Systems (ORMS) Technical Committee, the Public Key Infrastructure Adoption (PKIA) Technical Committee, the Security Joint Committee, and the Web Services Federation (WSFED) Technical Committee. [522]

OASIS also organizes two public conferences annually on open standards, one in Europe and one in North America. In September 2008, OASIS will host Open Standards Forum 2008: Security Challenges for the Information Society near London, England. The four-day event will provide an "opportunity for the security standards community (public sector, private sector and standards developing organizations) to come together to discuss current issues and challenges, strategic approaches, recent successes, and future outlooks." [523] Experts from organizations such as Vodafone and ENISA (see Chapter 4) will gather to present and discuss innovative security solutions for digital signatures, enterprise security, authentication, secure electronic invoicing, trust in networked systems, federated identity standards and technologies, and key management.[524]

5.4.11 Trans-European Research and Education Networking Association (TERENA)

The Trans-European Research and Education Networking Association (TERENA) is a forum that seeks to "collaborate, innovate, and share knowledge in order to foster the development of Internet technology, infrastructure and services to be used by the research and education community." [525] The following are TERENA's four core pillars of activities:

- "Providing an environment for fostering new initiatives in the European research networking community.
- Supporting joint European work in developing, evaluating, testing, integrating and promoting new networking, middleware and application technologies through the TERENA.
- Organizing conferences, workshops, and seminars for the exchange of information in the European research networking community, and pursuing knowledge transfer to less advanced networking organizations.
- Promoting members' interests by representing the common interests and opinions of the membership contacts with governments, funding bodies, industry, and other organizations." [526]

Although TERENA has a Technical Programme that focuses on lower layer technologies, security, middleware, mobility, voice and video collaboration, and the grid, [527] security work in TERENA is primarily conducted through the activities of TF-CSIRT (see subsection on European Incident Response). However, TERENA does list several projects related to Authentication and Authorization Infrastructure (AAI) elsewhere on its website.

"Eduroam," an educational secure network roaming infrastructure based on 802.1X and RADIUS technologies "allows users of participating [European] institutions to access a wireless LAN at other participants' locations using their home institution's credentials," and has been running successfully since 2003. TERENA also hosts frequent workshops on identity management and European CAMPUS Architecture Middleware Planning (EuroCAMP), in addition to a Research and Education Federations (REFEDS) program to analyze technical specifications and policies for interoperability of federations. [528]

TERENA's Server Certificate Service (SCS) "aims to provide low-cost 'pop-up free' server certificates for the National Regional and Education Networks (NRENs) and their constituency," and TACAR (TERENA Academic CA Repository), implemented in 2003, "offers a trustworthy solution to the problem of downloading root CA certificates" using Public Key Infrastructure. Finally, the TERENA Task Force on European Middleware Coordination and Collaboration (TF-EMC2) has provided a forum to discuss middleware issues and foster collaboration in the middleware arena since 2004.[529]

5.4.12 World Wide Web Consortium (W3C)

The World Wide Web Consortium (W3C) is an international consortium of public and private organizations devoted "to lead[ing] the World Wide Web to its full potential by developing protocols and guidelines that ensure long-term growth for the Web." W3C was created in 1994 by Tim Berners-Lee, one of the founders of the Web, to build international consensus around Web technologies. W3C also "engages in education and outreach, develops software, and serves as an open forum for discussion about the Web." [530]

W3C currently focuses on security research and development of security standards through the work of two specific working groups, the Web Security Context Working Group and the XML Specifications Maintenance Working Group. Both working groups fall under the umbrella W3C Security Activity Statement, most recently prepared for the W3C Advisory Committee Meeting in October 2008.[531]

The Web Security Context Working Group was created following a March 2006 W3C Workshop on Transparency and Usability of Web Authentication and was chartered "to specify a baseline set of security context information that should be accessible to Web users, and practices for the secure and usable presentation of this information, to enable users to come to a better understanding of the context that they are operating in when making trust decisions on the Web." The Web Security Context Working Group's primary contribution has been research on Web Security Context: User Interface Guidelines, Web Security Experience, Indicators, and Trust: Scope and Use Cases, and Web User Interaction: Threat Trees. [532]

The XML Security Specifications Maintenance Working Group, chartered "to address the specific issues surrounding Canonical XML, XML Signature, and the Decryption Transform for XML Signature with respect to interactions with the current XML environment," recently published an XML Signature Syntax and Processing (2nd Edition) W3C Recommendation[533] and is currently working to document best practices for XML Signature. Following completion of its work, a new XML Security Working Group will take on results from the September 2007 Workshop on Next Steps for the XML Security Specifications and additional work on XML Signature and XML Encryption standards. [534] The XML Signature Working Group, the XML Core Working Group, the XML Encryption Working Group, and the XML Key Management Working Group have also provided prior work on W3C Web Security research standards and initiatives. [535]

6 Making global cyberspace more secure...?

Security is becoming an increasingly important issue in the international landscape of cyberspace. Government, industry, and private citizens have become progressively more dependent on the Internet for information storage, data exchange, electronic commerce, social networking, gaming, electronic voting, banking, and professional advancement. With developments in technology and the increasing interconnectedness of global computer networks, the prevalence of information system bugs and vulnerabilities is growing and cyber threats are becoming more sophisticated, more diverse, more malicious, more effective, more affordable, and more readily available to hackers, organized criminals, rogue nations, and terrorists.

This study examines approximately seventy international, regional, nongovernmental, and private-public organizations with varying degrees of commitment to developing an ecosystem of safety and security in cyberspace. These organizations have focused their efforts on local and regional policy initiatives, international harmonization of laws, basic research and technological innovation, law enforcement, education and training, incident response, and propagation of secure ICTs. But are they doing it well? Are these organizations presenting practical, innovative, collaborative, and sustainable solutions to address cyberspace's security issues?

An initial study on the emergence of organizations working to secure cyberspace concluded in 2006 that, although many international initiatives were well underway, few metrics had been made publicly available to provide positive answers to these questions.[536] Two years later, though the landscape of cyber security has grown and evolved in many ways, organizations are still not producing readily available standardized metrics on the progress of their efforts. This recurring challenge is discussed in more detail below, following a brief analysis of new and existing organizations emerging in the international realm of cyber security.

6.1 Further Analysis of Recent Advances in Cyber Security

International intergovernmental organizations like the United Nations (UN) and the North American Treaty Organization (NATO) are pursuing collaborative solutions to the various challenges presented by malicious online activity. The UN, primarily through the work of the International Telecommunication Union (ITU), has established subcommittees and working parties to address the security challenges facing today's information society. Such organizations include the International Telecommunication Union's Telecommunication Development Sector (ITU-D) and Corporate Strategy Division (CSD), as well as other affiliated organizations like the United Nations Office on Drugs and Crime (UNODC). In addition, the Organisation for Economic Co-operation and Development (OECD)'s Working Party on Information Security and Privacy (WPISP) has provided ongoing support to the security of cyberspace by advancing education and information sharing throughout member countries. Through the Group of Eight's (G8) 24/7 Network of Contacts for High-Tech Crime and the NATO Computer Incident Response Capability-Technical Centre (NCIRC-TC), constituent nations now have central contacts for cybercrime-related incidents. In addition, INTERPOL regional working parties provide cybercrime law enforcement training and educational opportunities in various regions around the world.

Regional intergovernmental organizations are also contributing to the global effort to secure cyberspace. The European Union (EU) Parliament has issued numerous cyber security declarations, resolutions, and communications, while the Council of Europe (COE) established one of the most widely recognized precedents in agreement on international cyber security policy – the Convention on Cybercrime. Other organizations throughout Europe are also active in addressing the challenges of cyber security. Such organizations include the Organization for Security and Co-operation in Europe (OSCE)'s Action against Terrorism Unit (ATU), the European Telecommunications Standards Institute (ETSI), the European Committee for Standardization (CEN), and the Information and Communications Technologies Standards Board (ICTSB). Incident response for cyber attacks in Europe has been coordinated primarily by the European Task Force on Computer Security Incident Response Teams (TF-CSIRT), and Europol's High-Tech Crime Centre has released ongoing threat assessments and other comprehensive reports on regional cybercrime.

The Asia-Pacific region is also making progress in information security and cybercrime prevention. The Asia Pacific Economic Cooperation (APEC)'s Telecommunications and Information Working Group (TEL), through the work of the Security and Prosperity Steering Group (SPSG), issued the Shanghai Declaration in 2002 and has since hosted various conferences and workshops on network security and cyber terrorism. The Association of Southeast Asian Nations (ASEAN)'s Regional Forum (ARF) and Telecommunications and IT Ministers (TELMIN) have focused on promoting cooperation and harmonization of security policies, as well as capacity-building and Computer Emergency Response Team (CERT) cooperation throughout the Asia-Pacific region. In addition, the Asia-Pacific Telecommunity (APT), the United Nations Economic and Social Commission for Asia and the Pacific (UN ESCAP), and China-Japan-Korea (CJK) have contributed in the areas of network security and electronic commerce. The Asia Pacific Computer Emergency Response Team (APCERT) has now taken an active role in coordinating CSIRTs throughout the region.

The Organization of American States (OAS) and the Latin American Cooperation of Advanced Networks (CLARA) have facilitated numerous programs and initiatives towards enhancing cyber security in the Americas. In particular, the Inter-American Telecommunication Commission (CITEL) is now active throughout the region in promoting development of secure telecommunications and combating fraud. The CLARA Security Task Force (GT-Seg) and the OAS Inter-American Committee Against Terrorism (CICTE) have begun coordinating regional incident response and Computer Security Incident Response Team (CSIRT) collaboration. OAS's Group of Governmental Experts on Cyber-Crime has encouraged law enforcement cooperation in the region through various training programs and technical workshops.

Non-governmental and private-public organizations are also emerging to address global threats to cyberspace. Anti-spam advocates such as Spamhaus, the London Action Plan, CAUCE, and the StopSpamAlliance are active in promoting public awareness, cooperation, and international action against spam. Similarly, the Anti-Phishing Working Group, the International Botnet Task Force, and the Anti-Spyware Coalition have become leaders in combating phishing attacks, botnets, and malware, respectively.

The Forum of Incident Response and Security Teams (FIRST), primarily through the efforts of its 195 CSIRT teams across forty-three countries, has been active in promoting international cyber security incident response and prevention. [537] Organizations such as the Authentication & Online Trust Alliance (AOTA), the International Chamber of Commerce (ICC), and the World Information Technology and Services Alliance (WITSA) have sponsored frequent events to promote security policy and public awareness. Research, development, and standardization of cyber security products and protocols have also become a common objective among emerging international non-governmental organizations (NGOs) and private-public partnerships, including the 3rd Generation Partnership Project (3GPP), the Cooperative Association for Internet Data Analysis (CAIDA), the Institute of Electrical and Electronics Engineers (IEEE), the Internet Engineering Task Force (IETF), the Internet Society (ISOC), and the European Research and Education Networking Association (TERENA). These organizations are developing advanced security technologies, including standards in authentication, identity management, cryptography, key management, and biometrics – often competitive with those solutions produced exclusively by the private sector.

It is not possible to formulate any specific conclusions on the overall landscape of international cyber security without adequate metrics to measure the success of the organizations cataloged in this book. Further research is needed to identify standard international metrics to address this issue. Such metrics could include the following: the number of the number of cyber criminals arrested and prosecuted as a direct result of an organization's efforts; the number of incidents successfully handled by CSIRTs; the number of companies an organization saves from cyber catastrophe; and the amount of spam, phishing, or other forms of unsolicited communications intercepted or otherwise prevented from reaching its intended target.[538] These metrics will not only indicate the effectiveness of the organizations working to secure cyberspace, but will also help countries and the private sector to identify and focus further efforts on successful mechanisms and initiatives. Such metrics would also cast light on issues that are not being adequately addressed by current organizations.

For many of the organizations described in this book, a sufficient amount of time has not yet elapsed to adequately quantify the impact of their efforts. Many of these organizations have only been around for a decade or less – some have been around for only a few years. Even those organizations that have been around for awhile are not producing sufficient metrics on cyber security activity. In order to make any arguable claim about the success of any of these organizations, more time is necessary. Very few studies, if any, have yet to be conducted measuring the success of these organizations. As cyber security itself is only a relatively new field in the public realm of ICTs, further research must be done to quantify (or qualify) the impact of cyber security efforts focusing on the availability of networked systems, the privacy of personal information, the confidentiality of network communication, the authenticity and integrity of transmitted data, and the credibility of information systems by the general Internet user population.

6.2 Opportunities for Further Research

This study focused on selected categories of organizations which were previously given a general lack of attention and exposure in the emerging international landscape of cyber security. Due to the sheer number of global institutions that currently exist in the field, this study specifically excluded several categories of organizations that, while still an integral part of the collective ecosystem of safety and security, have historically received more attention and publicity. Further research, therefore, is required on the contribution of these organizations in order to accurately evaluate the overall progress of global cyber security efforts: privately funded organizations (e.g. Microsoft, Secure Computing); pure research-driven academic institutions; organizations serving a strictly national objective (e.g. national security agencies, such as the United States Department of Homeland Security or the Korean Security Agency); ICT infrastructure maintenance, operations, and administration organizations (e.g. ICANN, ARIN, LACNIC); and publicly hosted, open, non-affiliated conferences on newly discovered system vulnerabilities and innovative attack models (e.g. Black Hat, Hacker Con, etc).

Further research is also necessary on the progress of ICT security programs and initiatives throughout Africa and the Middle East – two regions with rapidly advancing ICT infrastructures that may lack the necessary security mechanisms to protect against international cyber threats. Many regional intergovernmental organizations provide publicly accessible resources and tools to promote cyber security research, policy, incident response, and education in member countries. Those in Africa and the Middle East, however, are not currently as advanced. For example, because they are still developing and may not yet have the necessary ICT infrastructure to promote their work, a majority of organizations identified in these regions do not currently host publicly accessible websites which can be easily translated, and some do not even have websites at all. Over time, due to the capacity-building efforts of international policymaking bodies like the ITU, communities across Africa and the Middle East will likely have access to the same cyber security tools and resource as those already advancing in other regions.

As a relatively new topic in the field of information security, critical information infrastructure protection (CIIP) poses an opportunity for both public and private sectors to collaborate on prevention, mitigation, and response to cyber threats against critical infrastructure control systems and interconnected information networks (e.g. power plants, water supply, pipelines, etc). The increasing dependence of these critical supply chain infrastructures on automated control systems and networked technologies creates new vulnerabilities that can be easily exploited by hackers, cyber terrorists, and rogue nations with enough incentive, resource, and skill to perpetrate malicious wide-scale attacks. Although many of the organizations presented in this book do have current programs related to research and education in the field of information infrastructure protection, a bulk of research on CIP is currently conducted by national security organizations which deserve further attention. In addition, because of the transnational nature of CIIP, more attention should also be given to international and regional intergovernmental organizations with specific commitments to incident response and prevention.

The current international landscape of cyber security is advancing. However, as the technologies supporting the Internet become more sophisticated, so too will the threats against them. Great challenges lie ahead in the ongoing pursuit of privacy, integrity, authenticity, and availability of global information. As such, the multitude of organizations identified in this study will continue to be tasked with responding to the growing number of threats posed by those seeking to inflict financial, political, psychological, and physical damage online. At present, the quantity of publicly available information that would help us more effectively benchmark and evaluate their progress remains inadequate. In order to help make a more measureable impact in the global ecosystem of safety and security in cyberspace, these organizations are going to have to start producing more substantial metrics and defining success in greater terms.

Appendix A – Abbreviations

3GPP – 3rd Generation Partnership Program
AAI - Authentication and Authorization Infrastructure
ABA – American Bar Association
AEPD – Spanish Data Protection Agency
AGB – Alliance for Global Business
ALM – Application Layer Multicast
AOTA – Authentication and Online Trust Alliance
APCAUCE – Asia Pacific Coalition Against Unsolicited Commercial Email
APCERT – Asia Pacific Computer Emergency Response Team
APEC – Asia-Pacific Economic Cooperation
APT – Asia-Pacific Telecommunity
APWG – Anti-Phishing Working Group
ARF – ASEAN Regional Forum
ARIN – American Registry for Internet Numbers
ARPANET – Advanced Research Projects Agency Network
ARW – (SPS) Advanced Research Workshop
ASC – Anti-Spyware Coalition
ASEAN – Association of Southeast Asian Nations
ASPWP – (INTERPOL) Asia-South Pacific Working Party
ASRG – (IRTF) Anti-Spam Research Group
ASTC – (CJK) Action Strategy on Trilateral Cooperation
ATRC – ASEAN Telecommunications Regulators Council
BIAC – (OECD) Business and Industry Advisory Committee
BIAS - Biometric Identity Assurance Services
BTF – International Botnet Task Force
CA – Certificate Authority
CAIDA - Cooperative Association for Internet Data Analysis
CAUBE.AU – Coalition Against Unsolicited Bulk Email, Australia
CAUCE – Coalition Against Unsolicited Commercial Email
CAUCE AU – CAUCE Australia
CAUCE NA – CAUCE North America
CCIF – (OISSF) Computer Crime Investigation Framework
CCMS – (NATO) Committee on the Challenges of Modern Society
ccTLD – Country Code Top Level Domain
CDCP – (COE) European Committee on Crime Problems
CEB – (UN) Chief Executives Board
CeCOS – (APWG) Counter eCrime Operations Summit
CEENet – Central and Eastern European Networking Association
CEN – European Committee for Standardization

CENELEC – European Committee for Electrotechnical Standardization
CEP – (FIRST) Corporate Executive Program
CERIAS - Center for Education and Research in Information Assurance and Security
CERT/CC – (Carnegie Mellon University) Computer Emergency Response Team/Coordination Center
CFRG – (IRTF) Crypto Forum Research Group
CIA – Confidentiality, Integrity, and Availability
CICTE – (OAS) Inter-American Committee Against Terrorism
CIIP – Critical Information Infrastructure Protection
CIP – Critical Infrastructure Protection
CISTP – (Georgia Institute of Technology) Center for International Strategy, Technology, and Policy
CITEL – (OAS) Inter-American Committee on Telecommunications
CJK – China-Japan-Korea
CLARA – Latin American Cooperation of Advanced Networks
CNSA – (European Union) Contact Network of Spam Authorities
COE – Council of Europe
CORDIS – (EU) Community Research and Development Information Service
CPTDA – Central Police Training and Development Authority
CSD – (ITU) Corporate Strategy Division
CSF – (IEEE) Computer Security Foundations
CSIRT – Computer Security Incident Response Team
CSPRI – Cyber Security Policy and Research Institute
CTF – (OISSG) Capture the Flag
CTTF – (APEC) Counter Terrorism Task Force
CULT – (EU) Committee on Culture and Education
CYB – (ITU) ICT Applications and Cybersecurity Division
DARPA – (United States). Defense Advanced Research Projects Agency
DDoS – Distributed Denial of Service
DKIM – DomainKeys Identified Mail
DNSBL – (Spamhaus) Domain Name System Blacklist
DRM – Data Rights Management
DROP – (Spamhaus) Don't Route or Peer List
DSS-X - Digital Signature Services eXtended
EBITT – (ICC) Commission on E-Business, IT, and Telecoms
ECEG – (WCO) Expert Group on Electronic Crime
EKMI - Enterprise Key Management Infrastructure
EMEA – (ISOC) Europe, Middle East, Africa
ENISA – (EU) European Network and Information Security Agency
ESCAP – (UN) Economic and Social Commission for Asia and the Pacific
eTEN – (EU) Trans-European Networks for Telecommunications
ETSI – European Telecommunications Standards Institute
EU – European Union

EuroCAMP – (TERENA) European CAMPUS Architecture Middleware Planning

Europol – European Police Office

EV SSL – Extended Validation Secure Sockets Layer

EWI – EastWest Institute

EWPITC – (INTERPOL) European Working Party on Information Technology Crime

FBI – (United States) Federal Bureau of Investigation

FIRST – Forum of Incident Response and Security Teams

FP7 – (EU) Seventh Research Framework Programme

FSTC – Financial Services Technology Consortium

FTC – (United States) Federal Trade Commission

G8 – Group of Eight

GCA – (ITU) Global Cybersecurity Agenda

GIAC – Global Information Assurance Certification

GIIC – Global Information Infrastructure Commission

GIP – (WITSA) Global Internet Project

GPPC – (WITSA) Global Public Policy Conference

GSE – GIAC Security Expert

GSM – Global System for Mobile (Communication)

GSMA – GSM Association

GT-CSIRT – CLARA Computer Security Incident Response Team

GT-Seg – CLARA Security Task Force ("Grupo de Trabajo Seguridad")

GTISC – Georgia Tech Information Security Center

GUIDEC – (ICC) General Usage for International Digitally Ensured Commerce

HIPAA – (United States) Health Insurance Portability and Accountability Act

HLEG – (ITU) High-Level Experts Group on Cybersecurity

IA – Information Assurance

IACR – International Association for Cryptologic Research

IAB – (IETF) Internet Architecture Board

iCAUCE – CAUCE International

ICC – International Chamber of Commerce

ICCP – (OECD) Committee for Information, Computer, and Communications Policy

ICSTD – (ESCAP) Information, Communication, and Space Technology Division

ICT – Information and Communication Technology

ICTSB – Information and Communications Technologies Standards Board

IDM – Identity Management

IEC – International Electrotechnical Commission

IEEE – Institute of Electrical and Electronics Engineers

IETF – Internet Engineering Task Force

IFIP – International Federation for Information Processing

IGF – (UN) Internet Governance Forum

ILETS – International Law Enforcement Telecommunications Seminar

IMPACT – International Multilateral Partnership Against Cyber-Terrorism
INTERPOL – International Criminal Police Organization
INTUG – International Telecommunications Users Group
IP – Internet Protocol
IRSG – (IRTF) Internet Research Steering Group
IRTF – Internet Research Task Force
ISC – (SANS) Internet Storm Center
ISO – International Organization for Standardization
ISOC – Internet Society
ISOI – Internet Security Operations and Intelligence
ISP – Internet Service Provider
ISSAF – (OISSG) Information Systems Security Assessment Framework
ISSS – (CEN) Information Society Standardization System
ITCIM – Information Technology Crime Investigation Manual
ITRE – (EU) Committee on Industry, Research and Energy
ITU – International Telecommunication Union
ITU-D – ITU Telecommunication Development Sector
ITU-R – ITU Radiocommunication Sector
ITU-T– ITU Telecommunication Standardization Sector
IWG - Interagency Working Group on Information and Communication Technology
LAP – London Action Plan
LAWPITC – (INTERPOL) Latin America Working Party on Information Technology Crime
LI – Lawful Interception
LIBE – (EU) Committee on Civil Liberties, Justice and Home Affairs
MAAWG – Messaging Anti-Abuse Working Group
MAS – Mobile Application Security
METI – (Japan) Ministry of Economy, Trade, and Industry
MLAT – Mutual Legal Assistance Treaty
Mob Opts – (IRTF) IP Mobility Optimizations Research Group
NII – National Information Infrastructure
NATO – North Atlantic Treaty Organization
NCIRC TC – NATO Computer Incident Response Capability Technical Centre
NCRP – (INTERPOL) National Central Reference Points
NDSS – (ISOC) Network and Distributed System Security Symposium
NERN – (TERENA) National Regional and Education Network
NGN – Next Generation Networks
NGO – Non-Governmental Organization
NIS – Network and Information Security
NISSG – (ICTSB) Network and Information Security Steering Group
NPIA – National Policing Improvement Agency
NREN – (TERENA) National Regional and Education Network
NSM - Network Security Monitoring

OAS – Organization of American States
OASIS – Organization for the Advancement of Structured Information Standards
OECD – Organization for Economic Co-operation and Development
OISSG – Open Information Systems Security Group
ORMS - Open Reputation Management Systems
OSCE - Organization for Security and Co-operation in Europe
P2P RG – (IRTF) Peer-to-Peer Research Group
PBL – (Spamhaus) Policy Block List
PCI – Payment Card Industry
PITA - Pacific Island Telecommunications Association
PKI – Public Key Infrastructure
PKIA - Public Key Infrastructure Adoption
POLCYB – Society for the Policing of Cyberspace
PREDICT – Protected Repository for the Defense of Infrastructure Against Cyber Threats
QEI – Quiet Enjoyment Infrastructure
REFEDS – (TERENA) Research and Education Federations
REMJA – (OAS) Ministers of Justice or Ministers or Attorneys General of the Americas
ROKSO – (Spamhaus) Register of Known Spam Operations
RTIR – (TF-CSIRT) Request Tracker for Incident Response
S3 - (3GPP) Technical Specification Group on Services and System Aspects – Working Group 3
SAG-S – (ISO/IEC/ITU-T) Strategic Advisory Group on Security
SANS – SysAdmin, Audit, Network, Security (Institute)
SAP – Security and Awareness Program
SAS – (GSMA) Security Accreditation Scheme
SBL – Spamhaus Block List
SCADA – Supervisory Control and Data Acquisition
SCS – (TERENA) Server Certification Service
SDSC – (CAIDA) San Diego Supercomputing Center
SEF – (OISSG) Security Essentials Framework
SEINIT – (ISOC-EMEA) Security Expert Initiative
SIDF – Sender ID Framework
SIG – (FIRST) Special Interest Group
SME – Small and Medium Enterprise
SMTP – Simple Mail Transfer Protocol
SPS – (NATO) Science for Peace and Security Committee
SPSG – (APEC) Security & Prosperity Steering Group
SPU – (ITU) Strategy & Policy Unit
SSI – (SANS) Software Security Institute
STEP – Security Training and Education Program
SSA – StopSpamAlliance
TACAR – TERENA Academic CA Repository

TC LI – (ETSI) Technical Committee on Lawful Interception
TC11 – (IFIP) Technical Committee Eleven
TCPA – (United States) Telephone Consumer Protection Act
TCSP – (IEEE) Technical Committee on Security and Privacy
TECS – The Europol Computer System
TEL – (APEC) Telecommunications and Information Working Group
TELMIN – (APEC/ASEAN) Telecommunications and Information Ministers and Leaders
TELSOM – (ASEAN) Telecommunications Senior Officials' Meeting
TERENA – Trans-European Research and Education Networking Association
TF-CSIRT – (TERENA) European Task Force on Computer Security Incident Response Teams
TF-EMC2 – (TERENA) Task Force on European Middleware Coordination and Collaboration
TI – (TF-CSIRT) Trusted Introducer
TMB – (ISO) Technical Management Board
TOPSI – (INTERPOL) Training and Operational Standards Initiative for High-Tech Crime
TRANSITS – (TF-CSIRT) Training of Network Security Incident Teams
TSG SA WG3 – (3GPP) Technical Specification Group on Services and System Aspects – Working Group 3
UN – United Nations
UN-GAID – United Nations Global Alliance for ICT and Development
UNAFEI – United Nations Asia & Far East Institute for the Prevention of Crime and the Treatment of Offenders
UNCTAD – United Nations Conference on Trade and Development
UNESCO – United Nations Educations, Scientific and Cultural Organization
UNODA – United Nations Office for Disarmament Affairs
UNODC – United Nations Office on Drugs and Crime
VoIP – Voice-over-IP
VWG – (ARF) Virtual Working Group
W3C – World Wide Web Consortium
WCC – (IFIP) World Computer Congress
WCIT – (WITSA) World Congress on Information and Technology
WCO – World Customs Organization
WG-AII – (TELSOM) Working Group on ASEAN Information Infrastructure
WITSA – World Information Technology and Services Alliance
WPISP – (OECD) Working Party on Information Security and Privacy
WSC – (WCO/EWI) Worldwide Security Conference
WSFED - Web Services Federation
WSIS – World Summit on the Information Society
WS-SX - Web Services Secure Exchange
WTO – World Trade Organization
WTSA – (ITU) World Trust Signatories Association

WTSA-04 – (ITU) 2004 World Telecommunication Standardization Assembly
WTSA-08 – (ITU) 2008 World Telecommunication Standardization Assembly
XACML - eXtensible Access Control Markup Language
XBL – (Spamhaus) Exploits Block List
XSPA - Cross-Enterprise Security and Privacy Authorization

Appendix B – Convention on Cybercrime CETS No.: 185

The following chart lists member and non-member states of the Council of Europe that have signed or ratified the Convention on Cybercrime as of August 1, 2008.

Member States of the Council of Europe

States	Signature	Ratification	Entry into force	Notes	R.	D.	A.	T.	C.	O.
Albania	23/11/2001	20/6/2002	1/7/2004				X			
Andorra										
Armenia	23/11/2001	12/10/2006	1/2/2007							
Austria	23/11/2001									
Azerbaijan	30/6/2008				X	X	X			
Belgium	23/11/2001									
Bosnia and Herzegovina	9/2/2005	19/5/2006	1/9/2006				X			
Bulgaria	23/11/2001	7/4/2005	1/8/2005		X	X				
Croatia	23/11/2001	17/10/2002	1/7/2004							
Cyprus	23/11/2001	19/1/2005	1/5/2005							
Czech Republic	9/2/2005									
Denmark	22/4/2003	21/6/2005	1/10/2005		X		X	X		
Estonia	23/11/2001	12/5/2003	1/7/2004				X			
Finland	23/11/2001	24/5/2007	1/9/2007		X	X	X			
France	23/11/2001	10/1/2006	1/5/2006		X	X	X			
Georgia	1/4/2008									
Germany	23/11/2001									
Greece	23/11/2001									
Hungary	23/11/2001	4/12/2003	1/7/2004		X	X	X			
Iceland	30/11/2001	29/1/2007	1/5/2007		X		X			
Ireland	28/2/2002									
Italy	23/11/2001	5/6/2008	1/10/2008				X			
Latvia	5/5/2004	14/2/2007	1/6/2007		X		X			
Liechtenstein										
Lithuania	23/6/2003	18/3/2004	1/7/2004		X	X	X			
Luxembourg	28/1/2003									
Malta	17/1/2002									
Moldova	23/11/2001									

State	Signature	Ratification	Entry into force	Notes	R.	D.	A.	T.	C.	O.
Monaco										
Montenegro	7/4/2005			55						
Netherlands	23/11/2001	16/11/2006	1/3/2007				X	X		
Norway	23/11/2001	30/6/2006	1/10/2006		X	X	X			
Poland	23/11/2001									
Portugal	23/11/2001									
Romania	23/11/2001	12/5/2004	1/9/2004				X			
Russia										
San Marino										
Serbia	7/4/2005			55						
Slovakia	4/2/2005	8/1/2008	1/5/2008		X	X	X			
Slovenia	24/7/2002	8/9/2004	1/1/2005				X			
Spain	23/11/2001 r									
Sweden	23/11/2001									
Switzerland	23/11/2001									
the former Yugoslav Republic of Macedonia	23/11/2001	15/9/2004	1/1/2005				X			
Turkey										
Ukraine	23/11/2001	10/3/2006	1/7/2006		X		X			
United Kingdom	23/11/2001									

Non-member States of the Council of Europe

States	Signature	Ratification	Entry into force	Notes	R.	D.	A.	T.	C.	O.
Canada	23/11/2001									
Costa Rica										
Japan	23/11/2001									
Mexico										
Philippines										
South Africa	23/11/2001									
United States	23/11/2001	29/9/2006	1/1/2007		X	X	X			

Total number of signatures not followed by ratifications:	22
Total number of ratifications/accessions:	23

Notes: (55) Date of signature by the state union of Serbia and Montenegro.
a: Accession - s: Signature without reservation as to ratification - su: Succession - r: Signature "ad referendum".

R.: Reservations - D.: Declarations - A.: Authorities - T.: Territorial Application - C.: Communication - O.: Objection.

Source: Treaty Office on http://conventions.coe.int, (CETS No. 185)

Index

References

[1] Nain D, Donaghy N, Goodman S (2008) The International Landscape of Cyber Security. In: Straub D, Goodman S, Baskerville R (ed) Information Security: Policy, Processes, and Practices. M.E.Sharpe, New York

[2] Miniwatts Marketing Group (2008) World Internet Users and Population Statistics. Internet Usage Statistics: The Internet Big Picture. http://www.internetworldstats.com/stats.htm. Accessed 30 June 2008

[3] Nain D, Donaghy N, Goodman S (2008) The International Landscape of Cyber Security. In: Straub D, Goodman S, Baskerville R (ed) Information Security: Policy, Processes, and Practices. M.E.Sharpe, New York

[4] Cerf V (2007) Emerging Cyber Security Threats and Countermeasures. GTISC Fall 2007 Security Summit Webcast. http://www.gtisc.gatech.edu/securitysummit1007_webcast.html. Accessed 31 July 2008

[5] Nain D, Donaghy N, Goodman S (2008) The International Landscape of Cyber Security. In: Straub D, Goodman S, Baskerville R (ed) Information Security: Policy, Processes, and Practices. M.E.Sharpe, New York

[6] Nain D, Donaghy N, Goodman S (2008) The International Landscape of Cyber Security. In: Straub D, Goodman S, Baskerville R (ed) Information Security: Policy, Processes, and Practices. M.E.Sharpe, New York

[7] The European Union (2002) Communication from the Commission to the Council, the European Parliament, the Economic and Social Committee and the Committee of the Regions: Creating a Safer Information Society by Improving the Security of Information Infrastructures and Combating Computer-related Crime. Commission of the European Communities. http://www.usdoj.gov/criminal/cybercrime/intl/EUCommunication.0101.pdf. Accessed 04 August 2008

[8] Organisation for Economic Co-operation and Development (1986) Computer-related crime: analysis of legal policy. Paris, France

[9] United Nations (1990) Eighth United Nations Congress on the Prevention of Crime and the Treatment of Offenders. General Assembly. http://www.un.org/documents/ga/res/45/a45r121.htm. Accessed 07 December 2007

[10] United Nations (1990) Eighth United Nations Congress on the Prevention of Crime and the Treatment of Offenders. General Assembly. http://www.un.org/documents/ga/res/45/a45r121.htm. Accessed 07 December 2007

[11] Organization for Economic Co-operation and Development (1992) Recommendation of the Council concerning guidelines for the security of information systems. GD(92)10. Paris, France

[12] Nain D, Donaghy N, Goodman S (2008) The International Landscape of Cyber Security. In: Straub D, Goodman S, Baskerville R (ed) Information Security: Policy, Processes, and Practices. M.E.Sharpe, New York

[13] Schjolberg S (2005) Law Comes to Cyberspace. Cybercrime Law. http://www.cybercrimelaw.net/documents/UN_Bangkok_05.htm. Accessed 17 July 2007

[14] International Telecommunication Union (2008) ITU implementing Action Line C5. http://www.itu.int/osg/csd/cybersecurity/WSIS/. Accessed 04 August 2008

[15] International Telecommunication Union (2006) Basic Information: About WSIS. World Summit on the Information Society, Geneva 2003 – Tunis 2005. http://www.itu.int/wsis/basic/about.html. Accessed 27 July 2007

[16] International Telecommunication Union (2006) Basic Information: About WSIS. World Summit on the Information Society, Geneva 2003 – Tunis 2005. http://www.itu.int/wsis/basic/about.html. Accessed 27 July 2007

[17] International Telecommunication Union (2006) Basic Information: About WSIS. World Summit on the Information Society, Geneva 2003 – Tunis 2005. http://www.itu.int/wsis/basic/about.html. Accessed 27 July 2007

[18] International Telecommunication Union (2008) ITU implementing Action Line C5. http://www.itu.int/osg/csd/cybersecurity/WSIS/. Access 04 August 2008

[19] International Telecommunication Union (2006) ITU WSIS Thematic Meeting on Cybersecurity. http://www.itu.int/osg/spu/cybersecurity/2005/index.phtml. Accessed 04 August 2008

[20] International Telecommunication Union (2008) Stocktaking: General Information. World Summit on the Information Society. http://www.itu.int/wsis/stocktaking. Accessed 04 August 2008

[21] International Telecommunication Union (2006) Golden Book: Stakeholder Commitments and Initiatives. World Summit on the Information Society. http://www.itu.int/wsis/goldenbook/. Accessed 04 August 2008

[22] International Telecommunication Union (2008) First Meeting for WSIS Action Line C5: Building Confidence and Security in the Use of ICTs. http://www.itu.int/osg/csd/cybersecurity/WSIS/1stMeeting.html. Accessed 04 August 2008

[23] International Telecommunication Union (2008) Second Meeting for WSIS Action Line C5: Building Confidence and Security in the Use of ICTs. http://www.itu.int/osg/csd/cybersecurity/WSIS/2ndMeeting.html. Accessed 04 August 2008

[24] International Telecommunication Union (2008) Meeting Report. 3rd Facilitation Meeting for WSIS Action Line C5: Building confidence and security in the use of ICTs. http://www.itu.int/osg/csd/cybersecurity/WSIS/3rd_meeting_docs/WSIS_Action_Line_C5_Meeting_Report_June_2008.pdf. Accessed 04 August 2008

[25] International Telecommunication Union (2007) Executive Summary. World Information Society Report 2007: Beyond WSIS.

http://www.itu.int/osg/spu/publications/worldinformationsociety/2007/WISR07-summary.pdf. Accessed 04 August 2008

[26] International Telecommunication Union (2007) Chapter 5: Challenges to building a safe and secure Information Society. 2007 World Information Society Report: Beyond WSIS. http://www.itu.int/osg/spu/publications/worldinformationsociety/2007/WISR07-chapter5.pdf. Accessed 04 August 2008

[27] Electronic Privacy Information Center (2005) The Council of Europe's Convention on Cybercrime. http://www.epic.org/privacy/intl/ccc.html. Accessed 25 July 2007

[28] United Stated Department of Justice (2003) Council of Europe Convention on Cybercrime: Frequently Asked Questions and Answers. Computer Crime and Intellectual Property Section. http://www.usdoj.gov/criminal/cybercrime/COEFAQs.htm. Accessed 28 July 2007

[29] Nain D, Donaghy N, Goodman S (2008) The International Landscape of Cyber Security. In: Straub D, Goodman S, Baskerville R (ed) Information Security: Policy, Processes, and Practices. M.E.Sharpe, New York

[30] Council of Europe (2008) Convention on Cybercrime CETS No.: 185. http://conventions.coe.int/Treaty/Commun/ChercheSig.asp?NT=185&CM=8&DF=&CL=ENG. Accessed 01 August 2008

[31] United Nations (2008) Chapter 1 – How the UN Works. UN in Brief. http://www.un.org/Overview/uninbrief/chapter1_intro.html. Accessed 04 August 2008

[32] International Telecommunication Union (2008) ITU's History. About IT. http://www.itu.int/net/about/history.aspx. Accessed 04 August 2008

[33] Nain D, Donaghy N, Goodman S (2008) The International Landscape of Cyber Security. In: Straub D, Goodman S, Baskerville R (ed) Information Security: Policy, Processes, and Practices. M.E.Sharpe, New York

[34] International Telecommunication Union (2007) ITU Activities related to Cybersecurity. http://www.itu.int/cybersecurity/. Accessed 05 August 2007

[35] International Telecommunication Union (2007) Cybersecurity Gateway http://www.itu.int/cybersecurity/gateway/index.html. Accessed 05 August 2007

[36] International Telecommunication Union (2006) Final Acts of the Plenipotentiary Conference (Antalya, 2006). http://www.itu.int/ITU-D/cyb/cybersecurity/docs/security-related-extracts-pp-06.pdf. Accessed 04 August 2008

[37] International Telecommunication Union (2006) Final Acts of the Plenipotentiary Conference (Antalya, 2006). http://www.itu.int/ITU-D/cyb/cybersecurity/docs/security-related-extracts-pp-06.pdf. Accessed 04 August 2008

[38] International Telecommunication Union (2007) Regional Workshop on Frameworks for Cybersecurity and Critical Information Infrastructure Protection. http://www.itu.int/ITU-D/cyb/events/2007/hanoi/index.html. Accessed 04 August 2008

[39] International Telecommunication Union (2007) Regional Workshop on Frameworks for Cybersecurity and Critical Information Infrastructure Protection. http://www.itu.int/ITU-D/cyb/events/2007/hanoi/index.html. Accessed 04 August 2008

[40] International Telecommunication Union (2007) Regional Workshop on Frameworks for Cybersecurity and Critical Information Infrastructure Protection. http://www.itu.int/ITU-D/cyb/events/2007/buenos-aires/index.html. Accessed 03 November 2007

[41] International Telecommunication Union (2007) Regional Workshop on Frameworks for Cybersecurity and Critical Information Infrastructure Protection. http://www.itu.int/ITU-D/cyb/events/2007/praia/index.html. Accessed 04 August 2008

[42] International Telecommunication Union (2008) Regional Workshop on Frameworks for Cybersecurity and Critical Information Infrastructure Protection. http://www.itu.int/ITU-D/cyb/events/2008/doha/index.html. Accessed 04 August 2008

[43] International Telecommunication Union (2004) Cybersecurity Symposium. http://www.itu.int/ITU-T/worksem/cybersecurity/more.html. Accessed 04 August 2008

[44] International Telecommunication Union (2006) Cybersecurity Symposium II. http://www.itu.int/ITU-T/worksem/cybersecurityII/index.html. Accessed 04 August 2008

[45] International Telecommunication Union (2004) Assembly outlines future global standards-setting. http://www.itu.int/newsroom/press_releases/2004/25.html. Accessed 04 August 2008

[46] International Telecommunication Union (2004) Resolution 50 – Cybersecurity. World Telecommunication Standardization Assembly. http://www.itu.int/ITU-T/wtsa/resolutions04/Res50E.pdf. Accessed 04 August 2008

[47] International Telecommunication Union (2004) Resolution 51 – Combating spam. World Telecommunication Standardization Assembly. http://www.itu.int/ITU-T/wtsa/resolutions04/Res51E.pdf. Accessed 04 August 2008

[48] International Telecommunication Union (2004) Resolution 52 – Countering spam by technical means. World Telecommunication Standardization Assembly. http://www.itu.int/ITU-T/wtsa/resolutions04/Res52E.pdf. Accessed 04 August 2008

[49] International Telecommunication Union (2008) World Telecommunication Standardization Assembly (WTSA-08). http://www.itu.int/ITU-T/wtsa-08/. Accessed 04 August 2008

[50] International Telecommunication Union (2007) ITU-T News log –Security. http://www.itu.int/ITU-T/newslog/CategoryView,category,Security.aspx. Accessed 04 August 2008

[51] International Telecommunication Union (2007) Cybersecurity related activities in ITU-T. http://www.itu.int/ITU-T/newslog/CategoryView,category,Security.aspx. Accessed 04 August 2008

[52] International Telecommunication Union (2007) ICT Security Standards Roadmap. ITU-T Study Group 17. http://www.itu.int/ITU-T/studygroups/com17/ict/. Accessed 04 August 2008

[53] International Telecommunication Union (2007) ICT Applications and Cybersecurity Division (CYB). http://www.itu.int/ITU-D/cyb/. Accessed 12 July 2007

[54] International Telecommunication Union (2007) 2007 Cybersecurity Guide for Developing Countries. http://www.itu.int/ITU-D/cyb/newslog/2007+Cybersecurity+Guide+For+Developing+Countries.aspx. Accessed 12 July 2007

[55] International Telecommunication Union (2008) Cybersecurity. ICT Applications and Cybersecurity Division. http://www.itu.int/ITU-D/cyb/cybersecurity/index.html. Accessed 04 August 2008

[56] International Telecommunication Union (2007) ITU ICT Eye. http://www.itu.int/ITU-D/icteye/Default.aspx. Accessed 14 August 2007

[57] International Telecommunication Union (2008) ITU Botnet Mitigation Toolkit. ICT Applications and Cybersecurity Division. http://www.itu.int/ITU-D/cyb/cybersecurity/projects/botnet.html. Accessed 04 August 2008

[58] International Telecommunication Union (2008) ITU National Cybersecurity/CIIP Self-Assessment Toolkit. ICT Applications and Cybersecurity Division. http://www.itu.int/ITU-D/cyb/cybersecurity/projects/readiness.html. Accessed 04 August 2008

[59] International Telecommunication Union (2007) ITU Toolkit for Cybercrime Legislature. ICT Applications and Cybersecurity Division. http://www.itu.int/ITU-D/cyb/cybersecurity/projects/cyberlaw.html. Accessed 04 August 2008

[60] International Telecommunication Union (2008) Regional Cybersecurity Forum for Europe and CIS. ICT Applications and Cybersecurity Division. http://www.itu.int/ITU-D/cyb/events/2008/sofia/index.html. Accessed 04 August 2008

[61] International Telecommunication Union (2006) WTDC-06: Doha Declaration. http://www.itu.int/ITU-D/wtdc06/DohaDeclaration.html. Accessed 04 August 2008

[62] International Telecommunication Union (2006) World Telecommunication Development Conference (WTDC-06). http://www.itu.int/ITU-D/wtdc06/. Accessed 04 August 2008

[63] International Telecommunication Union (2006) Programme 3: e-Strategies and ICT applications. Doha Action Plan. http://www.itu.int/ITU-D/cyb/publications/2006/dohaactionplanprogramme3.pdf. Accessed 04 August 2008

[64] International Telecommunication Union (2007) Cybersecurity related activities in ITU-R. http://www.itu.int/cybersecurity/ITU-R/. Accessed 04 August 2008

[65] International Telecommunication Union (2008) Corporate Strategy. Office of the Secretary-General. http://www.itu.int/osg/csd/. Accessed 04 August 2008

[66] International Telecommunication Union (2008) ITU Corporate Strategy News log. Office of the Secretary General http://www.itu.int/cybersecurity/watch/. Accessed 04 August 2008

128

[67] International Telecommunication Union (2007) World Telecommunication and Information Society Day ceremony honours three laureates. http://www.itu.int/newsroom/press_releases/2007/10.html. Accessed 03 November 2007

[68] International Telecommunication Union (2008) Global Cybersecurity Agenda. Corporate Strategy Division. http://www.itu.int/osg/csd/cybersecurity/gca/. Accessed 04 August 2008

[69] ETH Zurich (prepared for the International Telecommunication Union) (2007) A Generic National Framework for Critical Information Infrastructure Protection (CIIP). Center for Security Studies. http://www.itu.int/ITU-D/cyb/cybersecurity/docs/generic-national-framework-for-ciip.pdf. Accessed 04 August 2008

[70] International Telecommunication Union (2003) Document WSIS-03/GENEVA/DOC/4-E. Declaration of Principles – Building the Information Society: a global challenge in the new Millennium. World Summit on the Information Society. http://www.itu.int/wsis/docs/geneva/official/dop.html. Accessed 04 August 2008

[71] International Telecommunication Union (2004) Chairman's Report. ITU Thematic Meeting on Countering Spam. World Summit on the Information Society. http://www.itu.int/wsis/docs/geneva/official/dop.html. Accessed 04 August 2008

[72] International Telecommunication Union (2004) Chairman's Report. ITU Thematic Meeting on Countering Spam. World Summit on the Information Society. http://www.itu.int/wsis/docs/geneva/official/dop.html. Accessed 04 August 2008

[73] International Telecommunication Union (2008) Countering Spam and Related Threats. ICT Applications and Cybersecurity Division. http://www.itu.int/ITU-D/cyb/cybersecurity/spam.html. Accessed 04 August 2008

[74] International Telecommunication Union (2006) ITU WSIS Thematic Meeting on Cybersecurity. http://www.itu.int/osg/spu/cybersecurity/2005/index.phtml. Accessed 04 August 2008

[75] International Telecommunication Union (2008) Financial Aspects of Network Security: Malware and Spam. ITU-T Study Group 3. Geneva, Switzerland. http://www.itu.int/ITU-D/cyb/presentations/2008/bauer-financial-aspects-spam-malware-april-2008.pdf. Accessed 04 August 2008

[76] The World Trust Signatories Association (2008) The World e-Trust Initiative. http://trustsig.org/index.html. Accessed 04 August 2008

[77] International Telecommunication Union (2005) Report on the WSIS Stocktaking. World Summit on the Information Society. http://www.itu.int/wsis/docs2/tunis/off/5.pdf. Accessed 04 August 2008

[78] The World Trust Signatories Association (2008) The Two Sides of WTSA. http://trustsig.org/aboutus.html. Accessed 04 August 2008

[79] Osmio (2008) Osmio History. Osmio: The AuthentiCity. http://osmio.org/about_history.html. Accessed 04 August 2008

[80] United Nations Office of Drugs and Crime (2008) About UNODC. http://www.unodc.org/unodc/en/about-unodc/index.html. Accessed 04 August 2008

[81] International Telecommunication Union (2007) Abstracts for Meeting Presentations. 2nd WSIS Action Line C5 Facilitation Meeting. http://www.itu.int/osg/csd/cybersecurity/pgc/2007/events/presentation_abstracts.phtml. Accessed 04 August 2008

[82] United Nations Office of Drugs and Crime (2007) International cooperation in the prevention, investigation, prosecution and punishment of fraud, the criminal misuse and falsification of identity and related crimes. Commission on Crime Prevention and Criminal Justice. United Nations, Economic and Social Council. http://www.unodc.org/pdf/crime/15_commission/study-on-fraud-and-the-criminal-misuse-and-falsification-of-identity-first-draft.pdf. Accessed 04 August 2008

[83] United Nations Office of Drugs and Crime (2007) Cyber Crime Training Programme. http://www.unodc.org/india/cyber_crime_kerala.html. Accessed 04 August 2008

[84] United Nations Office on Drugs and Crime (2004) Report on the Expert Group Meeting on Technical Assistance Guidelines. http://www.unodc.org/pdf/crime/terrorism/seminars/Cape_Town_Report_Expert_Group_Meeting.doc. Accessed 04 August 2008

[85] United Nations Office on Drugs and Crime (2006) Criminal justice assessment toolkit. Policing: Crime Investigation. http://www.unodc.org/pdf/criminal_justice/CRIME_INVESTIGATION.pdf. Accessed 04 August 2008

[86] United Nations Office on Drugs and Crime (2007) Global congress tackles financial and Internet fraud. UNODC e-Newsletter. http://www.unodc.org/newsletter/en/perspectives/no03/page011.html. Accessed 04 August 2008

[87] United Nations (2008) United Nations Office for Disarmament Affairs (UNODA). Peace and Security Through Disarmament. http://disarmament.un.org/dda.htm. Accessed 01 August 2008

[88] Chellany B (2001) Revolution in Information Technology and its Impact on Security. The Asian Pacific Region: Evolution of the Scope of Security and Disarmament in the 21st Century. United Nations Conference on Disarmament Issues. http://disarmament.un.org/RCPD/pdf/plen2b.pdf. Accessed 01 August 2008

[89] Organisation for Economic Co-operation and Development (1992) Recommendation of the Council concerning guidelines for the security of information systems. OECD/GD(92)10. Paris, France

[90] Organisation for Economic Co-operation and Development (2007) The Development of Policies for the Protection of Critical Information Infrastructure. Working Party on Information Security and Privacy. Seoul, Korea. http://www.oecd.org/dataoecd/25/10/40761118.pdf. Accessed 01 August 2008

[91] Organisation for Economic Co-operation and Development (2005) The Promotion of a Culture of Security for Information Systems and Networks in OECD Countries. http://www.oecd.org/dataoecd/16/27/35884541.pdf. Accessed 25 July 2007

[92] Organisation for Economic and Co-operation and Development (2004) Summary of Responses to the Survey on the Implementation of the OECD Guidelines for the Security of Information Systems and Networks: Towards a Culture of Security. Working Party on Information Security and Privacy. http://www.olis.oecd.org/olis/2003doc.nsf/LinkTo/NT00007272/$FILE/JT00169904.PDF. Accessed 04 August 2008

[93] Organisation for Economic Co-operation and Development (2005) The Promotion of a Culture of Security for Information Systems and Networks in OECD Countries. http://www.oecd.org/dataoecd/16/27/35884541.pdf. Accessed 25 July 2007

[94] Organisation for Economic Co-operation and Development (2004) OECD Global Forum on Information Systems and Networks Security: Towards a Global Culture of Security. http://www.oecd.org/dataoecd/54/32/31453706.pdf. Accessed 04 August 2008

[95] Organisation for Economic Co-operation and Development (2005) APEC-OECD Workshop on Security of Information Systems and Networks: Summary. http://www.oecd.org/document/46/0,3343,en_2649_34255_36862382_1_1_1_1,00.html. Accessed 04 August 2008

[96] Organisation for Economic Co-operation and Development (2008) Culture of Security for information systems and networks. http://www.oecd.org/sti/cultureofsecurity. Accessed 04 August 2008

[97] Organisation for Economic Co-operation and Development (2008) What is the Working Party on Information Security and Privacy? Culture of Security for information and networks. http://www.oecd.org/document/46/0,3343,en_2649_34255_36862382_1_1_1_1,00.html. Accessed 04 August 2008

[98] Organisation for Economic Co-operation and Development (2007) APEC-OECD Workshop on Malware. http://www.oecd.org/dataoecd/37/60/38738890.pdf. Accessed 04 August 2008

[99] Organisation for Economic Co-operation and Development (2007) OECD Workshop on Digital Identity Management (IDM). http://www.oecd.org/sti/security-privacy/idm. Accessed 04 August 2008

[100] Organisation for Economic Co-operation and Development (2007) Report of the OECD Workshop on Digital Identity Management. http://www.oecd.org/dataoecd/30/52/38932095.pdf. Accessed 04 August 2008

[101] Organization for Economic Co-operation and Development (2008) Malicious Software (Malware): A Security Threat to the Internet Economy. OECD Ministerial Meeting on the Future of the Internet Economy. Seoul, Korea. http://www.oecd.org/dataoecd/53/34/40724457.pdf. Accessed 04 August 2008

[102] North Atlantic Treaty Organization (2007) Cyber Terrorism - A Serious Threat To Peace and Security in the 21st Century. Science for Peace and Security (SPS). http://www.nato.int/science/news/2007/n070702b.htm. Accessed 22 July 2007

[103] North Atlantic Treaty Organization (2002) Vulnerability of the Interconnected Society. NATO CCMS Short-Term Project: Final Report. Oslo, Norway.

http://www.nato.int/science/publication/nation_funded/doc/262-VIS%20Final%20Rep-Oct%202002.pdf. Accessed 03 August 2008

[104] Cerf V, Kahn R (1999) What Is The Internet (And What Makes It Work). Corporation for National Research Initiatives. http://www.cnri.reston.va.us/what_is_internet.html. Accessed 04 August 2008

[105] North Atlantic Treaty Organization (2002) Vulnerability of the Interconnected Society. NATO CCMS Short-Term Project: Final Report. Oslo, Norway. http://www.nato.int/science/publication/nation_funded/doc/262-VIS%20Final%20Rep-Oct%202002.pdf. Accessed 03 August 2008

[106] North Atlantic Treaty Organization (2008) Defending against cyber attacks. http://www.nato.int/issues/cyber_defence/index.html. Accessed 04 August 2008

[107] Michaels J (2007) NATO mulling safety against cyber attacks. USA Today. http://www.usatoday.com/news/world/2007-06-14-cyberattacks_N.htm. Accessed 04 August 2008

[108] Tallinn newsroom (2007) Seven states wish to participate in NATO center for cyber defense in Estonia. Estonian Embassy in Washington. http://www.estemb.org/news/aid-953. Accessed 12 December 2007

[109] North Atlantic Treaty Organization (2008) Defending against cyber attacks: What does this mean in practice? http://www.nato.int/issues/cyber_defence/practice.html. Accessed 04 August 2008

[110] North Atlantic Treaty Organization (2008) Defending against cyber attacks. http://www.nato.int/issues/cyber_defence/index.html. Accessed 04 August 2008

[111] North Atlantic Treaty Organization (2008) Defending against cyber attacks: What does this mean in practice? http://www.nato.int/issues/cyber_defence/practice.html. Accessed 04 August 2008

[112] North Atlantic Treaty Organization (2006) NATO Information Assurance Product Catalogue. http://nato-cat.softbox.co.uk/Pages/Home.aspx. Accessed 22 July 2007

[113] North Atlantic Treaty Organization (2007) Cyber terrorism – a serious threat to peace and security in the 21st century. Science for Peace and Security (SPS). http://www.nato.int/science/news/2007/n070702b.htm. Accessed 22 July 2007

[114] The World Bank (2008) Tables of Final Results 2005 International Comparison Program. http://siteresources.worldbank.org/ICPINT/Resources/ICP_final-results.pdf. Accessed 04 August 2008

[115] Group of Eight (2004) Background on the G8. Meeting of G8 Justice and Home Affairs Ministers. http://www.usdoj.gov/criminal/cybercrime/g82004/g8_background.html. Accessed 23 July 2007

[116] Schulzki-Haddouti C (1999) We also want to make a guide for other countries. Telepolis. http://jya.com/g8-charney.htm. Accessed 04 August 2008

132

[117] Group of Eight (2004) Background on the G8. Meeting of G8 Justice and Home Affairs Ministers. http://www.usdoj.gov/criminal/cybercrime/g82004/g8_background.html. Accessed 23 July 2007

[118] World Customs Organization (2008) About Us. http://www.wcoomd.org/home_about_us.htm. Accessed 04 August 2008

[119] World Customs Organization (2008) Electronic Crime. Responsibilities. http://www.wcoomd.org/home_wco_topics_epoverviewboxes_responsibilities_epelectroniccr ime.htm. Accessed 04 August 2008

[120] World Customs Organization (2008) The WCO Expert Group on Electronic Crime (ECEG). Meetings. http://www.wcoomd.org/home_wco_topics_epoverviewboxes_meetings_epeceg.htm. Accessed 04 August 2008

[121] The EastWest Institute (2008) Worldwide Security Conference Demands Effective Strategies. EastWest Institute Worldwide Security Conference. http://www.ewi.info/pdf/MediaAttachment65.pdf. Accessed 04 August 2008

[122] United States Department of Justice (2005) G8 24/7 high tech contact points invitation. http://www.cybersecuritycooperation.org/moredocuments/24%20Hour%20Network/24%207 %20invitation.pdf. Accessed 23 July 2007

[123] Schulzki-Haddouti C (1999) We also want to make a guide for other countries. Telepolis. http://jya.com/g8-charney.htm. Accessed 04 August 2008

[124] United States Department of Justice (2005) G8 24/7 high tech contact points invitation. http://www.cybersecuritycooperation.org/moredocuments/24%20Hour%20Network/24%207 %20invitation.pdf. Accessed 23 July 2007

[125] INTERPOL (2008) Information Technology Crime. http://www.interpol.int/Public/TechnologyCrime/default.asp. Accessed 04 August 2008

[126] INTERPOL (2002) European Working Party on Information Technology Crime: Terms of Reference. http://www.interpol.int/public/TechnologyCrime/WorkingParties/Europe/TermsOfRef.asp. Accessed 04 August 2008

[127] INTERPOL (2008) European Working Party on Information Technology Crime. Regional Working Parties. http://www.interpol.int/Public/TechnologyCrime/WorkingParties/default.asp#europa. Accessed 04 August 2008

[128] INTERPOL (2007) Cyber-crime. Fact Sheets. http://www.interpol.int/Public/ICPO/FactSheets/FHT02.pdf. Accessed 04 August 2008

[129] INTERPOL (2008) European Working Party on Information Technology Crime. Regional Working Parties. http://www.interpol.int/Public/TechnologyCrime/WorkingParties/default.asp#europa. Accessed 04 August 2008

[130] INTERPOL (2005) Resolution of the Delegates to the INTERPOL's 5th Meeting of the INTERPOL Working Party on IT Crime. Regional Working Parties. http://www.interpol.int/Public/TechnologyCrime/WorkingParties/Africa/5thMeeting/Resolution.asp. Accessed 04 August 2008

[131] INTERPOL (2008) African Working Party on Information Technology Crime. Regional Working Parties. http://www.interpol.int/Public/TechnologyCrime/WorkingParties/Default.asp#africa. Accessed 04 August 2008

[132] INTERPOL (2008) Asia-South Pacific Working Party on Information Technology Crime (ASPWP). Regional Working Parties. http://www.interpol.int/Public/TechnologyCrime/WorkingParties/Default.asp#asia. Accessed 04 August 2008

[133] INTERPOL (2008) Latin America Working Party on Information Technology Crime (LAWPITC). Regional Working Parties. http://www.interpol.int/Public/TechnologyCrime/WorkingParties/Default.asp#latinamerica. Accessed 04 August 2008

[134] INTERPOL (2007) 1st International Cyber Crime Investigation Training Conference. http://www.interpol.int/public/TechnologyCrime/Conferences/1stCybConf/Conference.asp. Accessed 04 August 2008

[135] INTERPOL (2007) Cyber-crime. Fact Sheets. http://www.interpol.int/Public/ICPO/FactSheets/FHT02.pdf. Accessed 04 August 2008

[136] INTERPOL (2007) INTERPOL urges integrated global cyber-crime investigation network to combat online threat. INTERPOL Media Release. http://www.interpol.int/Public/ICPO/PressReleases/PR2007/PR200740.asp. Accessed 04 August 2008

[137] INTERPOL (2008) Information Technology Crime. http://www.interpol.int/Public/TechnologyCrime/default.asp. Accessed 04 August 2008

[138] INTERPOL (2005) Information security and crime prevention. http://www.interpol.int/Public/TechnologyCrime/CrimePrev/default.asp. Accessed 04 August 2008

[139] Statewatch (2001) G8 and ILETS discussed problems of 'data retention and implications of data protection legislation' in 1999. Statewide Observatory on Surveillance in Europe. S.O.S. Europe. http://www.statewatch.org/news/2001/may/03Denfopol.htm. Accessed 25 July 2007

[140] Statewatch (1999) ILETS '99 draft report. ILETS 1999. http://www.statewatch.org/news/2001/may/ILETS99-report.doc. Accessed 25 July 2007

[141] Statewatch (2001) G8 and ILETS discussed problems of 'data retention and implications of data protection legislation' in 1999. Statewide Observatory on Surveillance in Europe. S.O.S. Europe. http://www.statewatch.org/news/2001/may/03Denfopol.htm. Accessed 25 July 2007

[142] Statewatch (1999) ILETS '99 draft report. ILETS 1999. http://www.statewatch.org/news/2001/may/ILETS99-report.doc. Accessed 25 July 2007

[143] Third Generation Partnership Project (2002) Report of the 3GPP TSG SA WG3-LI (S3-LI) meeting #3/02 on lawful interception. Helsinki, Finland. http://www.3gpp.org/ftp/tsg_sa/WG3_Security/TSGS3_LI/2002_09_Helsinki/SeLI02_159_r eport%20from%203GPP%20TWG%20SA%20WG3%20LI%202002-09.pdf. Accessed 03 August 2008

[144] Europa (2007) Treaty of Maastricht on European Union. Activities of the European Union: Summaries of legislation. http://europa.eu/scadplus/treaties/maastricht_en.htm. Accessed 10 August 2008

[145] Europa (2008) Information Society and Media Directorate General. http://ec.europa.eu/dgs/information_society/see_more/index_en.htm#mission. Accessed 21 August 2008

[146] Europa (2008) Activities of the European Union – Information Society. http://europa.eu/pol/infso/index_en.htm. Accessed 19 August 2008

[147] European Parliament (2008) ITRE Industry, Research, and Energy. http://www.europarl.europa.eu/activities/committees/homeCom.do?body=ITRE&language=E N. Accessed 19 August 2008

[148] European Parliament (2008) LIBE Civil Liberties, Justice, and Home Affairs. http://www.europarl.europa.eu/activities/committees/homeCom.do?body=LIBE&language=E N. Accessed 19 August 2008

[149] European Parliament (2008) CULT Culture and Education. http://www.europarl.europa.eu/activities/committees/homeCom.do?body=CULT&language= EN. Accessed 19 August 2008

[150] Europa (2005) Information Security. Activities of the European Union: Summaries of legislation. http://europa.eu/scadplus/leg/en/lvb/l24121.htm. Accessed 10 August 2008

[151] European Commission (2002) Anti cybercrime legislation proposals on Council table. Freedom, Security, and Justice. http://ec.europa.eu/justice_home/fsj/crime/cybercrime/wai/fsj_crime_cybercrime_en.htm. Accessed 10 August 2008

[152] Europa (2005) Fight against cybercrime. Activities of the European Union: Summaries of legislation. http://europa.eu/scadplus/leg/en/lvb/l33193b.htm. Accessed 10 August 2008

[153] The European Union (2001) Communication from the Commission to the European Council, the European Parliament, the European Economic and Social Committee, and the Committee of the Regions. Commission of the European Communities. http://eur-lex.europa.eu/LexUriServ/LexUriServ.do?uri=COM:2001:0298:FIN:EN:PDF. Accessed 10 August 2008

[154] Europa (2006) Organised crime: contact points to combat high-tech crime. Activities of the European Union: Summaries of legislation. http://europa.eu/scadplus/leg/en/lvb/l33157.htm. Accessed 10 August 2008

[155] European Commission (2004) Fighting Cybercrime. Information Society. http://ec.europa.eu/information_society/policy/cybercrime/index_en.htm. Accessed 10 August 2008

[156] The European Union (2002) Council resolution of 28 January 2002 on a common approach and specific actions in the area of network and information security (2002/C 43/02). Official Journal of the European Communities. http://eur-lex.europa.eu/LexUriServ/LexUriServ.do?uri=OJ:C:2002:043:0002:0004:EN:PDF. Accessed 10 August 2008

[157] The European Union (2003) Council resolution of 18 February 2003 on a European approach towards a culture of network and information security (2003/C 48/01). Official Journal of the European Communities. http://eur-lex.europa.eu/LexUriServ/LexUriServ.do?uri=OJ:C:2003:048:0001:0002:EN:PDF. Accessed 10 August 2008

[158] European Commission (2005) Decisions. Information Society. http://ec.europa.eu/information_society/activities/sip/programme/decision/index_en.htm#SIAP1999. Accessed 10 August 2008

[159] European Commission (2008) Safer Internet Programme (2009-2013). Information Society. http://ec.europa.eu/information_society/activities/sip/programme/index_en.htm. Accessed 10 August 2008

[160] European Commission (2007) Confidentiality of communications – spyware, cookies. Information Society. http://ec.europa.eu/information_society/policy/ecomm/todays_framework/privacy_protection/spyware_cookies/index_en.htm. Accessed 10 August 2008

[161] Europa (2008) Data protection in the electronic communications sector. http://europa.eu/scadplus/leg/en/lvb/l24120.htm. Accessed 21 August 2008

[162] European Commission (2007) eEurope 2005: Trust. Information Society. http://ec.europa.eu/information_society/eeurope/2005/all_about/security/index_en.htm. Accessed 10 August 2008

[163] European Commission (2007) eEurope 2005: Trust. Information Society. http://ec.europa.eu/information_society/eeurope/2005/all_about/security/index_en.htm. Accessed 10 August 2008

[164] European Commission (2007) eEurope 2005: Trust. Information Society. http://ec.europa.eu/information_society/eeurope/2005/all_about/security/risk_preparedness_study_technology/index_en.htm. Accessed 10 August 2008

[165] European Commission (2007) eEurope 2005: Trust - Handbook. Information Society. http://ec.europa.eu/information_society/eeurope/2005/all_about/security/handbook/index_en.htm. Accessed 10 August 2008

[166] European Commission (2007) i2010 strategy – key documents: i2010 Communication. Information Society. http://ec.europa.eu/information_society/eeurope/i2010/key_documents/index_en.htm#i2010_Communication. Accessed 10 August 2008

136

[167] The European Union (2006) Communication from the Commission to the Council, the European Parliament, the European Economic and Social Committee and the Committee of the Regions: A strategy for a Secure Information Society- Dialogue, partnership, and empowerment. Commission of the European Communities. http://eur-lex.europa.eu/LexUriServ/LexUriServ.do?uri=COM:2006:0251:FIN:EN:PDF. Accessed 10 August 2008

[168] The European Union (2007) Communication from the Commission to the European Parliament, the Council, and the Committee of the Regions: Towards a general policy on the fight against cybercrime – Impact Assessment Report. Commission of the European Communities. http://ec.europa.eu/governance/impact/docs/ia_2007/sec_2007_0642_en.pdf. Accessed 31 October 2007

[169] The European Union (2007) Communication from the Commission to the European Parliament, the Council, and the Committee of the Regions: Towards a general policy on the fight against cybercrime. Commission of the European Communities. http://eur-lex.europa.eu/LexUriServ/site/en/com/2007/com2007_0267en01.pdf. Accessed 01 November 2007

[170] CORDIS (2008) ICT Challenge 1: Pervasive and Trusted Network and Service Infrastructures. Information and Communication Technologies. http://cordis.europa.eu/fp7/ict/programme/challenge1_en.html. Accessed 10 August 2008

[171] The European Union (2006) Communication from the Commission to the European Parliament, the Council, the European Economic and Social Committee and the Committee of the Regions: On Fighting spam, spyware and malicious software. Commission of the European Communities. http://eur-lex.europa.eu/LexUriServ/LexUriServ.do?uri=COM:2006:0688:FIN:EN:PDF. Accessed 10 August 2008

[172] StopSpamAlliance (2007) The EU Contact Network of Spam Authorities. http://stopspamalliance.org/?page_id=11. Accessed 10 August 2008

[173] The European Union (2004) Communication from the Commission to the European Parliament, the Council, the European Economic and Social Committee, and the Committee of the Regions: on unsolicited commercial communications or 'spam.' Commission of the European Communities. http://eur-lex.europa.eu/LexUriServ/LexUriServ.do?uri=COM:2004:0028:FIN:EN:PDF. Accessed 10 August 2008

[174] The European Union (2006) Communication from the Commission to the European Parliament, the Council, the European Economic and Social Committee and the Committee of the Regions: On Fighting spam, spyware and malicious software. Commission of the European Communities. http://eur-lex.europa.eu/LexUriServ/LexUriServ.do?uri=COM:2006:0688:FIN:EN:PDF. Accessed 10 August 2008

[175] The European Union (2006) Communication from the Commission to the European Parliament, the Council, the European Economic and Social Committee and the Committee of the Regions: On Fighting spam, spyware and malicious software. Commission of the European Communities. http://eur-

lex.europa.eu/LexUriServ/LexUriServ.do?uri=COM:2006:0688:FIN:EN:PDF. Accessed 10 August 2008

[176] Council of Europe (2008) About the Council of Europe. http://www.coe.int/T/e/Com/about_coe/. Accessed 21 August 2008

[177] Council of Europe (2008) Convention on Cybercrime. Treaty Summaries. http://conventions.coe.int/Treaty/en/Summaries/Html/185.htm. Accessed 10 August 2008

[178] Council of Europe (2008) The information society and human rights. Internet Governance Forum. http://www.coe.int/t/dc/files/events/internet/default_EN.asp. Accessed 10 August 2008

[179] Council of Europe (2005) Conclusions of the Council of Europe conference on fight against cybercrime. Note to Editors. http://www.coe.int/T/E/Com/Press/News/NoteRedac2005/20051213_cybercrime.asp. Accessed 10 August 2008

[180] Council of Europe (2006) Council of Europe releases organized crime assessment. Press Release – 051(2006). https://wcd.coe.int/ViewDoc.jsp?Ref=PR051(2006)&Sector=secDC&Language=lanEnglish&Ver=original&BackColorInternet=F5CA75&BackColorIntranet=F5CA75&BackColorLogged=A9BACE. Accessed 10 August 2008

[181] Council of Europe (2007) Conference Summary. *Octopus Interface conference on Cooperation against cybercrime.* http://www.coe.int/t/e/legal_affairs/legal_co-operation/combating_economic_crime/3_technical_cooperation/cyber/567%20IF%202007-d-sumconclusions1g%20Provisional.pdf. Accessed 10 August 2008

[182] Council of Europe (2007) Legislators and Experts Workshop on Cybercrime. Makati City, Philippines. http://www.coe.int/t/e/legal_affairs/legal_co%2Doperation/combating_economic_crime/3_Technical_cooperation/CYBER/567%20phil-d-programme%20(2%20oct%2007).pdf. Accessed 10 August 2008

[183] Council of Europe (2007) Recommendation CM/Rec(2007)16 of the Committee of Ministers to member states on measures to promote the public service value of the Internet. Committee of Ministers. http://www.coe.int/t/dg1/legalcooperation/economiccrime/cybercrime/T-CY/T-CY_2008_CMrec0711_en.PDF. Accessed 10 August 2008

[184] Council of Europe (2007) Freedom of expression and security on the Internet are not contradictory but complementing values in the information society. Rio de Janeiro, Brazil. http://www.coe.int/t/dc/press/news/20071114_news_EN.asp. Accessed 10 August 2008

[185] Council of Europe (2007) Cybercrime and Identity Fraud and Theft – Issues for Discussion. European Conference on identity fraud and theft, Panel 2: Cybercrime. http://www.coe.int/t/dg1/legalcooperation/economiccrime/cybercrime/cy%20activity_events_on_identity_theft/567%20port%20id-m-ws%20concept1a%20_11%20july%2007_.pdf. Accessed 10 August 2008

[186] Seger A (2007) Identity theft and the Convention on Cybercrime. UN ISPAC Conference on the Evolving Challenge of Identity-related Crime.

138

http://www.coe.int/t/dg1/legalcooperation/economiccrime/cybercrime/cy%20activity_events_
on_identity_theft/567%20UN%20id%20theft%20and%20CCC_en.pdf. Accessed 10 August
2008

[187] Council of Europe (2007) Cairo Declaration against Cybercrime 2007. Cairo, Egypt.
http://www.coe.int/t/e/legal_affairs/legal_co%2Doperation/combating_economic_crime/6_cy
bercrime/CairoDeclarationAgainstCC2007_EN.pdf. Accessed 10 August 2008

[188] Council of Europe (2007) Conclusions. Regional workshop on cybercrime legislation and
training   of   judges.   Plovdiv,   Bulgaria.
http://www.coe.int/t/dg1/legalcooperation/economiccrime/cybercrime/cy%20activity%20bul/
cy%20activity%20bul-d-conclusions_en.pdf. Accessed 10 August 2008

[189] Council of Europe (2008) Conference to propose landmark cybercrime guidelines to increase
co-operation between law enforcement and Internet service providers. Press release –
218(2008).
https://wcd.coe.int/ViewDoc.jsp?Ref=PR218(2008)&Language=lanEnglish&Ver=original&S
ite=DC&BackColorInternet=F5CA75&BackColorIntranet=F5CA75&BackColorLogged=A9
BACE. Accessed 10 August 2008

[190] Council of Europe (2008) Conference Conclusions. Octopus Interface conference on Cooperation   against   cybercrime.
http://www.coe.int/t/dg1/legalcooperation/economiccrime/cybercrime/cy%20activity%20Inte
rface2008/567_IF08-d-concl1c.pdf. Accessed

[191] Council of Europe (2008) Summary and Workplan 2008-2009. Project on Cybercrime.
http://www.coe.int/t/dg1/legalcooperation/economiccrime/cybercrime/cy%20Project/567-d-
summary%20and%20workplan%202008-2009a%20_29%20Jan%2008_en.pdf. Accessed 10
August 2008

[192] Anti-Phishing   Working   Group   (2008)   CeCOS   II.
http://www.antiphishing.org/events/2008_operationsSummit.html. Accessed 10 August 2008

[193] Organization for Security and Co-operation in Europe (2007) About OSCE.
http://www.osce.org/about/. Accessed 27 November 2007

[194] Organization for Security and Co-operation in Europe (2007) Secretariat: Action against Terrorism Unit. http://www.osce.org/atu/. Accessed 27 November 2007

[195] Organization for Security and Co-operation in Europe (2001) The Bucharest Plan of Action
for   Combating   Terrorism.   MC(9).DEC/1.
http://www.osce.org/documents/cio/2001/12/670_en.pdf. Accessed 10 August 2008

[196] Organization for Security and Co-operation in Europe (2004) Action Against Terrorism Unit.
http://www.osce.org/publications/atu/2004/11/13544_47_en.pdf. Accessed 27 November
2007

[197] Organization for Security and Co-operation in Europe (2004) Decision No. 3/04: Combating
the Use of the Internet for Terrorist Purposes. 2nd Day of the 12th Meeting.
http://www.osce.org/documents/mcs/2004/12/3906_en.pdf. Accessed 10 August 2008

[198] Organization for Security and Co-operation in Europe (2006) Decision No. 7/06: Countering the Use of the Internet for Terrorist Purposes. http://www.osce.org/documents/mcs/2006/12/22559_en.pdf. Accessed 27 November 2008

[199] Organization for Security and Co-operation in Europe (2007) OSCE Political Public-Private Partnership Conference: Partnership of State Authorities, Civil Society and the Business Community in Combating Terrorism. http://www.osce.org/documents/atu/2007/09/26118_en.pdf. Accessed 10 August 2008

[200] Organization for Security and Co-operation in Europe (2008) Press Release: Cyber threat on the rise as terrorists recruit computer specialists, says OSCE expert. Secretariat – Action against Terrorism Unit. http://www.osce.org/atu/item_1_30591.html. Accessed 10 August 2008

[201] The European Telecommunications Standards Institute (2007) About ETSI. http://www.etsi.org/WebSite/AboutETSI/AboutEtsi.aspx. Accessed 28 November 2007

[202] The European Telecommunications Standards Institute (2006) Annual report 2006. http://www.etsi.org/WebSite/document/aboutETSI/Annual_report/ETSI_AR_2007.pdf. Accessed 10 August 2008

[203] The European Telecommunications Standards Institute (2006) ETSI Future Security Workshop: The threats, risks, and opportunities. ETSI Future Security Workshop Overview. http://portal.etsi.org/securityworkshop/include/Presentations06/ETSI_Future_Security_Work shop_Output_Report.pdf. Accessed 10 August 2008

[204] The European Telecommunications Standards Institute (2007) Workshop Report. ETSI 2nd Security Workshop: Future Security. http://portal.etsi.org/securityworkshop/Presentations07/ETSI_2nd_Security_Workshop_Repo rt.pdf. Accessed 10 August 2008

[205] The European Telecommunications Standards Institute (2008) 3rd ETSI Security Workshop. http://portal.etsi.org/securityworkshop/Home.asp. Accessed 10 August 2008

[206] European Committee for Standardization (2008) About Us. http://www.cen.eu/cenorm/aboutus/index.asp. Accessed 10 August 2008

[207] European Committee for Standardization (2008) Focus Groups. ISSS (ICT). http://www.cen.eu/cenorm/sectors/sectors/isss/focus/index.asp. Accessed 10 August 2008

[208] European Committee for Standardization (2008) Security, Trust, and Data protection. ISSS (ICT). http://www.cen.eu/cenorm/sectors/sectors/isss/activity/securitytrustdpp.asp. Accessed 10 August 2008

[209] European Committee for Standardization (2008) Network and Information Security Focus Group. ISSS (ICT). http://www.cen.eu/cenorm/sectors/sectors/isss/activity/nis_fg.asp. Accessed 10 August 2008

[210] European Committee for Standardization (2003) Response from CEN and ETSI to the 'Communication from the Commission to the Council, the European Parliament, the European Economic and Social Committee of the Regions: Network and Information Security: Proposal for a European Policy Approach.'

140

http://www.cen.eu/cenorm/sectors/sectors/isss/activity/nisissuewithtoc1.pdf. Accessed 10 August 2008

[211] European Committee for Standardization (2008) Network and Information Security Focus Group. ISSS (ICT). http://www.cen.eu/cenorm/sectors/sectors/isss/activity/nis_fg.asp. Accessed 10 August 2008

[212] ICT Standards Board (2001) The Board's Terms of Reference. http://www.ictsb.org/ToR.htm. Accessed 10 August 2008

[213] ICT Standards Board (2007) Introduction. Network and Information Security Steering Group. http://www.ictsb.org/NISSG. Accessed 10 August 2008

[214] ICT Standards Board (2007) FINAL VERSION: Network and Information Security Standards Report. Network and Information Security Steering Group. http://www.ictsb.org/NISSG. Accessed 10 August 2008

[215] ICT Standards Board (2007) Introduction. Network and Information Security Steering Group. http://www.ictsb.org/NISSG. Accessed 10 August 2008

[216] International Telecommunication Union (2007) ICT Security Standards Roadmap. ITU-T Study Group 17. http://www.itu.int/ITU-T. Accessed 10 August 2008

[217] European Network and Information Security Agency (2006) CERT cooperation and its further facilitation by relevant stakeholders. http://www.enisa.europa.eu/cert_cooperation/pages/07_04.htm. Accessed 13 August 2007

[218] European Network and Information Security Agency (2006) Information Security Awareness Programs in the EU: Insight and Guidance for Member States. Information Package 2006. http://www.enisa.europa.eu/doc/pdf/deliverables/enisa_is_aw_programmes_eu.pdf. Accessed 10 August 2008

[219] European Network Information Security Agency (2006) Management Summary. CERT cooperation and its further facilitation by relevant stakeholders. http://www.enisa.europa.eu/cert_cooperation/pages/01.htm. Accessed 10 August 2008

[220] European Network Information Security Agency (2006) The Annual Report of the European Network and Information Security Agency. http://www.enisa.europa.eu/doc/pdf/general_report_2006.pdf. Accessed 30 October 2007

[221] European Commission (2007) Evaluation of the European Network and Information Security Agency. http://ec.europa.eu/dgs/information_society/evaluation/studies/s2006_enisa/docs/final_report.pdf. Accessed 31 October 2007

[222] European Network and Information Security Agency (2008) Press Releases. http://www.enisa.europa.eu/pages/02_01.htm. Accessed 10 August 2008

[223] European Network and Information Security Agency (2008) ENISA Work Programme for 2008 adopted: ENISA driving for impact. Press Release. http://www.enisa.europa.eu/pages/02_01_press_2007_11_21_wp_2008.html. Accessed 10 August 2008

[224] The Trans-European Research and Education Networking Association (2006) TF-CSIRT. http://www.terena.org/activities/tf-csirt/. Accessed 10 August 2008

[225] The Trans-European Research and Education Networking Association (2006) TF-CSIRT Activities. http://www.terena.org/activities/tf-csirt/activities.html. Accessed 10 August 2008

[226] The Trans-European Research and Education Networking Association (2005) Request Software for Incident Response (RTIR) Software to be Upgraded and Expanded. http://www.terena.org/news/archive/2005/news-rtir.pdf. Accessed 10 August 2008

[227] The Trans-European Research and Education Networking Association (2007) Annual Report 2006. http://www.terena.org/publications/files/Annual_Report_2006.pdf. Accessed 28 November 2007

[228] The Trans-European Research and Education Networking Association (2007) CSIRT Training. http://www.terena.org/activities/csirt-training/. Accessed 17 July 2007

[229] European Law Enforcement Cooperation (2007) Fact sheet on Europol 2007. http://www.europol.europa.eu/index.asp?page=facts&language=en. Accessed 10 August 2008

[230] Pollard L (2001) Concerns over Europol. An introduction to the history, operation, and future of Europol. http://www.people.ex.ac.uk/watupman/undergrad/pollard/html/concerns.htm. Accessed 10 August 2008

[231] European Law Enforcement Cooperation (2007) High-Tech Crimes Within the EU: Threat Assessment 2007. High Tech Crime Centre. http://www.europol.europa.eu/publications/Serious_Crime_Overviews/HTCThreatAssessment2007.pdf. Accessed 10 August 2008

[232] European Law Enforcement Cooperation (2007) EU Terrorist Situation and Trend Report 2007. http://www.europol.europa.eu/publications/EU_Terrorism_Situation_and_Trend_Report_TE-SAT/TESAT2007.pdf. Accessed 10 August 2008

[233] National Policing Improvement Agency (2007) High Tech Crime. http://www.npia.police.uk/en/5236.htm. Accessed 10 August 2008

[234] National Policing Improvement Agency (2007) High Tech Crime. http://www.npia.police.uk/en/5236.htm. Accessed 10 August 2008

[235] Asia-Pacific Economic Cooperation (2008) About APEC. http://www.apec.org/content/apec/about_apec.html. Accessed 10 August 2008

[236] Asia-Pacific Economic Cooperation (2008) Telecommunications and Information Working Group. http://www.apec.org/apec/apec_groups/working_groups/telecommunications_and_information.html. Accessed 01 November 2007

[237] South Eastern Europe Conference on Cyber Security Cooperation (2002) Recommendation by the APEC TELWG to SOM for an APEC Cybersecurity Strategy. http://www.cybersecuritycooperation.org/documents/APEC. Accessed 10 August 2008

[238] South Eastern Europe Conference on Cyber Security Cooperation (2002) Recommendation by the APEC TELWG to SOM for an APEC Cybersecurity Strategy. http://www.cybersecuritycooperation.org/documents/APEC. Accessed 10 August 2008

[239] Asia-Pacific Economic Cooperation (2007) Chair's Report. The 35th APEC Telecommunications and Information Working Group Meeting. http://www.apectelwg.org/jsp/download.jsp?seq=4679&board_id=GPA_TEL. Accessed 01 November 2007

[240] Asia-Pacific Economic Cooperation (2005) APEC Principles for Actions against Spam. Lima, Peru. http://www.apec.org/apec/ministerial_statements/sectoral_ministerial/telecommunications/2005/annex_e.html. Accessed 10 August 2008

[241] Asia-Pacific Economic Cooperation (2005) Guiding Principles for PKI-Based Approaches to Electronic Authentication (Annex D). The Sixth APEC Ministerial Meeting on the Telecommunications and Information Industry (TEMIN6). http://www.apec.org/apec/ministerial_statements/sectoral_ministerial/telecommunications/2005/annex_d.html. Accessed 10 August 2008

[242] Asia-Pacific Economic Cooperation (2007) Chair's Report. The 35th APEC Telecommunications and Information Working Group Meeting. http://www.apectelwg.org/jsp/download.jsp?seq=4679&board_id=GPA_TEL. Accessed 01 November 2007

[243] Asia-Pacific Economic Cooperation (2007) Chair's Report. The 35th APEC Telecommunications and Information Working Group Meeting. http://www.apectelwg.org/jsp/download.jsp?seq=4679&board_id=GPA_TEL. Accessed 01 November 2007

[244] Asia-Pacific Economic Cooperation (2008) Programme. APECTEL37. http://www.apectel37.jp/programme/index.html. Accessed 10 August 2008

[245] Asia-Pacific Economic Cooperation (2008) TEL Calendar. Telecommunications and Information Working Group. http://www.apectelwg.org/. Accessed 10 August 2008

[246] Asia-Pacific Economic Cooperation (2008) Current Activities. Counter Terrorism Task Force. http://www.apec.org/apec/apec_groups/som_committee_on_economic/som_special_task_groups/counter_terrorism.html. Accessed 10 August 2008

[247] Asia-Pacific Economic Cooperation (2008) Current Activities. Telecommunications and Information Working Group. http://www.apec.org/apec/apec_groups/som_committee_on_economic/working_groups/telecommunications_and_information.html. Accessed 10 August 2008

[248] Association of Southeast Asian Nations (2007) Overview. http://www.aseansec.org/64.htm. Accessed 28 November 2007

[249] Association of Southeast Asian Nations (2007) ASEAN Vision 2020. http://www.aseansec.org/1814.htm. Accessed 28 November 2007

[250] ASEAN Regional Forum (2004) Co-Chairs' Summary of the ARF Seminar on Cyber Terrorism. http://64.233.167.104/search?q=cache:u34DTd5pMXEJ:www.aseanregionalforum.org/LinkClick.aspx%3Ffileticket%3DPnZBQQf381w%253D%26tabid%3D66%26mid%3D403+ASEAN+Regional+Forum+(ARF). Accessed 10 August 2008

[251] KOREA.net (2007) The 4th ASEAN Regional Forum (ARF) Seminar on Cyber Terrorism to be Held. Government Press Releases. http://www.korea.net/News/News/NewsView.asp?serial_no=20071017024. Accessed 28 November 2007

[252] ASEAN Regional Forum (2008) August 2007 – December 2008. Schedule of Meetings & Events. http://www.aseanregionalforum.org/Calendar/tabid/172/Default.aspx. Accessed 10 August 2008

[253] ASEAN Regional Forum (2008) ARF Virtual Working Group (VWG) on Cyber Security and Cyber Terrorism. http://209.85.207.104/search?q=cache:ve16col_GbYJ:www1.apan-info.net/jiacg/RegionalForum/tabid/3368/DMXModule/11167/Command/Core_Download/Default.aspx%3FEntryId%3D11234+4th+ARF. Accessed 10 August 2008

[254] ASEAN Telecommunication Regulators' Council (2005) About the ATRC Working Group on Network Security. Working Groups. http://www.aseanconnect.gov.my/atrc/aboutAntiSpam.php?groupId=6. Accessed 28 November 2007

[255] ASEAN Telecommunication Regulators' Council (2005) Database for the Network Security Working Group. Working Groups. http://www.aseanconnect.gov.my/atrc/db_answer.php?id=7&groupId=6. Accessed 10 August 2008

[256] ASEAN Connect (2005) Telecommunications and IT Senior Officials Meeting (TELSOM). http://www.aseanconnect.gov.my/telsom/telsom.php. Accessed 28 November 2007

[257] ASEAN Connect (2005) About the ASEAN Information Infrastructure (WG AII) Working Group. Telecommunications and IT Senior Officials Meeting (TELSOM). http://www.aseanconnect.gov.my/telsom/wgAIIAbout.php?groupId=1. Accessed 28 November 2007

[258] ASEAN Connect (2005) About the ASEAN Information Infrastructure (WG AII) Working Group. Telecommunications and IT Senior Officials Meeting (TELSOM). http://www.aseanconnect.gov.my/telsom/wgAIIAbout.php?groupId=1. Accessed 28 November 2007

[259] ASEAN Connect (2005) Database for the ASEAN Information Infrastructure (WG AII) Working Group. Telecommunications and IT Senior Officials Meeting (TELSOM). http://www.aseanconnect.gov.my/telsom/db_answer.php?id=2&groupId=1. Accessed 10 August 2008

144

[260] Asia-Pacific Telecommunity (2008) Asia-Pacific Telecommunity. http://www.aptsec.org/apt/aptintro.html. Accessed 13 August 2007

[261] Asia Pacific Telecommunity (2005) Workshop on CERT Best Practices. http://www.aptsec.org/meetings/2004/cert/default.htm. Accessed 10 August 2008

[262] Asia Pacific Telecommunity (2005) Symposium on Network Security and Spam. http://www.aptsec.org/meetings/2005/NSS/default.htm. Accessed 10 August 2008

[263] Asia Pacific Telecommunity (2008) Symposium on Network Security/Eleventh APT Standardization Forum. http://www.aptsec.org/meetings/2006/ASTAP11/default.htm. Accessed 10 August 2008

[264] Asia Pacific Telecommunity (2008) Network Security and Spam. http://www.aptsec.org/links/NSS/Default.htm. Accessed 31 October 2007

[265] Asia-Pacific Telecommunity (2007) Asia Pacific Telecommunity – Spam Initiatives & Developments. http://www.aptsec.org/links/NSS/ASTAP07-FR12-PL-30_SPAM-Initiatives-in-APT. Accessed 10 August 2008

[266] Asia Pacific Telecommunity (2008) Strategic Plan of the APT – 2006-2008. http://www.aptsec.org/apt/aptStra.html. Accessed 31 October 2007

[267] United Nations Economic and Social Commission for Asia and the Pacific (2008) General Description. About Us. http://www.unescap.org/about/. Accessed 10 August 2008

[268] United Nations Economic and Social Commission for Asia and the Pacific (2008) Who are we? Information, Communication, and Space Technology Division. http://www.unescap.org/icstd/who_we_are.asp. Accessed 10 August 2008

[269] United Nations Economic and Social Commission for Asia and the Pacific (2002) Report of the Asia-Pacific Conference on Cybercrime and Information Security. Information, Communication, and Space Technology Division. http://www.unescap.org/icstd/cybercrime%20meeting/Report,%20list%20of%20participants%20and%20Draft%20Action%20Plan/Cybercrime%20report.doc. Accessed 10 August 2008

[270] United Nations Economic and Social Commission for Asia and the Pacific (2002) Annex 2: Draft Action Plan on Cybercrime and Information Security for the Asia-Pacific region. Information, Communication, and Space Technology Division. http://www.unescap.org/icstd/cybercrime%20meeting/Report,%20list%20of%20participants%20and%20Draft%20Action%20Plan/DRAFT%20ACTION%20PLAN%20final%20version%20.doc. Accessed 10 August 2008

[271] United Nations Economic and Social Commission for Asia and the Pacific (2008) Workshops and Seminars organised. http://www.unescap.org/icstd/policy/activities/. Accessed 10 August 2008

[272] The Regional Interagency Working Group on ICT (2008) Draft Report. Eleventh Meeting of the Regional Interagency Working Group on Information and Communication Technologies (ICT). http://www.aptsec.org/iwg/11th-IWG. Accessed 10 August 2008

[273] United Nations Economic and Social Commission for Asia and the Pacific (2008) Internet use for business development – an introductory set of training modules for policymakers. Information, Communication, and Space Technology Division. http://www.unescap.org/icstd/policy/publications/internet%2Duse%2Dfor%2Dbusiness%2D development/index.asp. Accessed 10 August 2008

[274] United Nations Economic and Social Commission for Asia and the Pacific (2008) Information Security for Economic and Social Development. Information, Communication, and Space Technology Division. http://www.unescap.org/icstd/policy/publications/information%2Dsecurity%2Dfor%2Decono mic%2Dand%2Dsocial%2Ddevelopment/. Accessed 10 August 2008

[275] Ministry of Foreign Affairs of the People's Republic of China (2004) The Progress Report of the Trilateral Cooperation Among the People's Republic of China, Japan, and the Republic of Korea. http://www1.fmprc.gov.cn/eng/topics/wenjiabaoASEANeng/t175842.htm. Accessed 10 August 2008

[276] MPHPT Communication News (2003) Third Meeting of China-Japan-Korea ICT Working Group at DG Level Concluded Successfully. http://www.soumu.go.jp/joho_tsusin/eng/Releases/NewsLetter/Vol14/Vol14_07/Vol14_07.p df. Accessed 28 November 2007

[277] Ministry of Foreign Affairs of the People's Republic of China (2004) The Progress Report of the Trilateral Cooperation among the People's Republic of China, Japan, and the Republic of Korea. http://www.fmprc.gov.cn/eng/wjb/zzjg/yzs/dqzzywt/t175822.htm. Accessed 28 November 2007

[278] Ministry of Foreign Affairs of the People's Republic of China (2004) The Progress Report of the Trilateral Cooperation among the People's Republic of China, Japan, and the Republic of Korea. http://www.fmprc.gov.cn/eng/wjb/zzjg/yzs/dqzzywt/t175822.htm. Accessed 28 November 2007

[279] Ministry of Foreign Affairs of the People's Republic of China (2004) The Progress Report of the Trilateral Cooperation among the People's Republic of China, Japan, and the Republic of Korea. http://www.fmprc.gov.cn/eng/wjb/zzjg/yzs/dqzzywt/t175822.htm. Accessed 28 November 2007

[280] MPHPT Communications News (2004) Further Promotion of Cooperation among China-Japan-Korea in ICT Field. http://www.soumu.go.jp/joho_tsusin/eng/Releases/NewsLetter/Vol15/Vol15_09/Vol15_09.p df. Accessed 10 August 2008

[281] MPHPT Communications News (2004) Further Promotion of Cooperation among China-Japan-Korea in ICT Field. http://www.soumu.go.jp/joho_tsusin/eng/Releases/NewsLetter/Vol15/Vol15_09/Vol15_09.p df. Accessed 10 August 2008

[282] Asia Pacific Computer Emergency Response Team (2008) Member Teams. http://www.apcert.org/about/structure/members.html. Accessed 10 August 2008

[283] Asia Pacific Computer Emergency Response Team (2008) Mission Statement. http://www.apcert.org/about/mission/index.html. Accessed 10 August 2008

[284] Asia Pacific Computer Emergency Response Team (2005) APCERT 2005 Annual Report. http://www.apcert.org/documents/pdf/annualreport2005.pdf. Accessed 01 November 2007

[285] Ingram G (2006) Welcome Letter. APCERT/CNCERT 2006 Conference. http://2006.cert.org.cn/en/invitation.html. Accessed 10 August 2008

[286] Asia Pacific Computer Emergency Response Team (2007) APCERT Meetings Programs 7th – 9th February 2007. http://www.niser.org.my/apcert/programs.html. Accessed 03 November 2007

[287] Asia Pacific Computer Emergency Response Team (2008) Overview. APCERT Conference 2008. http://apcert2008.hkcert.org/. Accessed 10 August 2008

[288] Asia Pacific Computer Emergency Response Team (2006) APCERT Shuts Down Malware Embedded Sites During Drill Exercise. APCERT Media Release. http://www.apcert.org/documents/pdf/APCERT. Accessed 03 November 2007

[289] Asia Pacific Computer Emergency Response Team (2006) APCERT Shuts Down Malware Embedded Sites During Drill Exercise. APCERT Media Release. http://www.apcert.org/documents/pdf/APCERT. Accessed 03 November 2007

[290] Nain D, Donaghy N, Goodman S (2008) The International Landscape of Cyber Security. In: Straub D, Goodman S, Baskerville R (ed) Information Security: Policy, Processes, and Practices. M.E.Sharpe, New York

[291] Asia-Pacific Economic Cooperation (2003) Protecting developing economies from cyber attack – assistance to build regional cyber security preparedness. APEC Media Release. http://www.apec.org/apec/news___media/2003_media_releases/180303_sin_protecting_deve loping_economies.html. Accessed 23 July 2007

[292] Organization of American States (2007) OAS History at a Glance. http://www.oas.org/. Accessed 25 June 2007

[293] Organization of American States (1997) Charter of the Organization of American States. Department of International Legal Affairs. http://www.oas.org/juridico/english/charter.html. Accessed 04 November 2007

[294] Organization of American States (2004) Adoption Of A Comprehensive Inter-American Strategy To Combat Threats To Cybersecurity: A Multidimensional And Multidisciplinary Approach To Creating A Culture Of Cybersecurity. General Assembly. http://www.oas.org/XXXIVGA/english/docs/approved_documents/adoption_strategy_comba t_threats_cybersecurity.htm. Accessed 10 August 2008

[295] Organization of American States (2005) International Conference on 'Cybercrime: A Global Challenge, A Global Response.' Hemispheric Cooperation in the Fight against Cyber-Crime. Office of Legal Cooperation. http://www.oas.org/juridico/english/cyber_conf_crime.htm. Accessed 30 October 2007

[296] Organization of American States (2007) What is CITEL? Inter-American Telecommunication Commission. http://citel.oas.org/what_is_citel.asp. Accessed 10 August 2008

[297] Organization of American States (2006) Declaration of San Jose. Inter-American Telecommunication Commission. http://www.citel.oas.org/assembly/Declaracion%20de%20San%20Jose_i.doc. Accessed 10 August 2008

[298] Organization of American States (2007) Rapporteur Group on Cybersecurity & Critical Infrastructure. Inter-American Telecommunication Commission. http://www.citel.oas.org/ccp1-tel/Cybersecurity.asp. Accessed 14 July 2007

[299] Organization of American States (2007) Rapporteur Group on Cybersecurity & Critical Infrastructure. Inter-American Telecommunication Commission. http://www.citel.oas.org/ccp1-tel/Cybersecurity.asp. Accessed 14 July 2007

[300] Organization of the American States (2005) The Blue Book: Telecommunication Policies for the Americas. Inter-American Telecommunication Commission. http://www.citel.oas.org/publications/azul-fin-r1c1_i.pdf. Accessed 30 October 2007

[301] Organization of American States (2008) Calendar 2008. Inter-American Telecommunication Commission. http://www.citel.oas.org/calendar_2008.asp. Accessed 10 August 2008

[302] Latin American Cooperation of Advanced Networks (2008) About CLARA: Objectives. http://www.redclara.net/en/01/02.htm. Accessed 21 July 2007

[303] Latin American Cooperation of Advanced Networks (2008) About CLARA: Objectives. http://www.redclara.net/en/01/02.htm. Accessed 21 July 2007

[304] Latin American Cooperation of Advanced Networks (2006) GT Seguridad: Presente y futuro. Reunión Técnica CLARA-TEC. http://gt-seg.seguridad.unam.mx/documentos/Security-Clara-Quito.pdf?PHPSESSID=323ea79b9787b4d26dcf246113fc1eb4. Accessed 10 August 2008

[305] Organization of American States (2006) Cyber Security. Inter-American Committee Against Terrorism. http://www.cicte.oas.org/Rev/En/Programs/CyberSecurity.asp. Accessed 10 August 2008

[306] Organization of American States (2006) Cyber Security- Upcoming and Recent Events. Inter-American Committee Against Terrorism. http://www.cicte.oas.org/Rev/EN/Events/CyberSecurity.asp. Accessed 10 August 2008

[307] Organization of American States (2008) 2008 Work Plan of the Inter-American Committee Against Terrorism. Inter-American Committee Against Terrorism. http://www.cicte.oas.org/Database_/CICTE. Accessed 10 August 2008

[308] Organization of American States (2007) OAS Advances on Computer Security Incident Response Teams. CICTE Newsletter 46. Inter-American Committee Against Terrorism. http://www.cicte.oas.org/rev/en/About/Newsletters/Informe_46_eng.pdf. Accessed 10 August 2008

[309] Organization of American States (2004) Draft Resolution: Adoption of a Comprehensive Inter-American Strategy to Combat Threats to Cybersecurity. Committee on Hemispheric Security. http://scm.oas.org/doc_public/ENGLISH/HIST_04/CP12893E04.doc. Accessed 10 August 2008

148

[310] Organization of American States (2006) Cyber Security- Upcoming and Recent Events. Inter-American Committee Against Terrorism. http://www.cicte.oas.org/Rev/EN/Events/CyberSecurity.asp. Accessed 10 August 2008

[311] Organization of American States (2006) II Cyber Security and Cyber Crime Workshop. Inter-American Committee Against Terrorism. http://www.cicte.oas.org/Rev/EN/Events/Cyber_Events/II_Workshop_MIAMI-2007.asp. Accessed 10 August 2008

[312] Organization of American States (2007) Declaration of Panama on the Protection of Critical Infrastructure in the Hemisphere in the Face of Terrorism. Inter-American Committee Against Terrorism. http://www.cicte.oas.org/Rev/En/Documents/Declarations/doc_dec_1_07_final_eng.pdf. Accessed 10 August 2008

[313] Latin American Cooperation of Advanced Networks (2006) GT Seguridad: Presente y futuro. Reunión Técnica CLARA-TEC. http://gt-seg.seguridad.unam.mx/documentos/Security-Clara-Quito.pdf?PHPSESSID=323ea79b9787b4d26dcf246113fc1eb4. Accessed 10 August 2008

[314] Latin American Cooperation of Advanced Networks (2006) GT Seguridad: Presente y futuro. Reunión Técnica CLARA-TEC. http://gt-seg.seguridad.unam.mx/documentos/Security-Clara-Quito.pdf?PHPSESSID=323ea79b9787b4d26dcf246113fc1eb4. Accessed 10 August 2008

[315] Organization of American States (2008) Group of Experts and Cybercrime: Background. Inter-American Cooperation Portal on Cyber-Crime. Office of Legal Cooperation. http://www.oas.org/juridico/english/cyber.htm. Accessed 30 October 2007

[316] Organization of American States (2006) Recommendations of the Fourth Meeting of the Group of Governmental Experts on Cyber-Crime. IV Meeting of the Group of Governmental Experts on Cyber-Crime. Meeting of the Ministers of Justice or Ministers or Attorneys General of the Americas. http://www.oas.org/juridico/english/cybGE_IVrec.doc. Accessed 30 October 2007

[317] Organization of American States (2007) Technical Workshops following the Fourth Meeting. Hemispheric Cooperation in the Fight against Cyber-Crime. Office of Legal Cooperation. http://www.oas.org/juridico/english/cyber_tech_wrkshp.htm. Accessed 30 October 2007

[318] Organization of American States (2007) Draft Agenda. V Meeting of the Group of Governmental Experts on Cyber-Crime. Meeting of the Ministers of Justice or Ministers or Attorneys General of the Americas. http://www.oas.org/juridico/spanish/Vagenda_en.pdf. Accessed 30 October 2007

[319] Council of Europe (2007) Convention on Cybercrime CETS No.: 185. http://conventions.coe.int/Treaty/Commun/ChercheSig.asp?NT=185&CM=8&DF=&CL=ENG. Accessed 14 August 2007

[320] Organization of American States (2007) Recommendations. V Meeting of the Group of Governmental Experts on Cyber-Crime. Meetings of Ministers of Justice or Ministers or Attor-

neys General of the Americas. http://www.oas.org/juridico/spanish/cyb_Vrec_en.doc. Accessed 10 August 2008

[321] Organization of American States (2008) Group of Experts and Cybercrime: Background. Inter-American Cooperation Portal on Cyber-Crime. Office of Legal Cooperation. http://www.oas.org/juridico/english/cyber.htm. Accessed 30 October 2007

[322] Coalition Against Unsolicited Commercial Email (2007) About CAUCE. http://www.cauce.org/about. Accessed 02 December 2007

[323] Coalition Against Unsolicited Commercial Email (2007) History. About CAUCE. http://www.cauce.org/about/history.html. Accessed 10 August 2008

[324] Coalition Against Unsolicited Commercial Email (2008) CAUCE. http://www.cauce.org/index.php. Accessed 10 August 2008

[325] London Action Plan (2006) The Plan in Detail. http://www.londonactionplan.org/?q=node/1. Accessed 03 November 2007

[326] London Action Plan (2005) L.A.P. holds Spam Enforcement Workshop. http://www.londonactionplan.org/?q=node/8. Accessed 10 August 2008

[327] London Action Plan (2007) 3rd Joint LAP-CNSA Workshop: Collaborative Ventures to Fight Online Threats. http://www.londonactionplan.org/?q=node/10. Accessed 03 November 2007

[328] London Action Plan (2007) 3rd Joint LAP-CNSA Workshop: Collaborative Ventures to Fight Online Threats. http://www.londonactionplan.org/?q=node/10. Accessed 03 November 2007

[329] Messaging Anti-Abuse Working Group (2007) About MAAWG. http://www.maawg.org/about/. Accessed 03 November 2007

[330] Messaging Anti-Abuse Working Group (2007) About MAAWG. http://www.maawg.org/about/. Accessed 03 November 2007

[331] Messaging Anti-Abuse Working Group (2007) Who Is In MAAWG? http://www.maawg.org/about/roster/. Accessed 03 November 2007

[332] Messaging Anti-Abuse Working Group (2007) MAAWG Attacks BotNets with Walled Garden Best Practices to Protect Users. http://www.maawg.org/news/maawg071024. Accessed 03 November 2007

[333] Messaging Anti-Abuse Working Group (2008) MAAWG Membership Information. http://www.maawg.org/about/join_us/. Accessed 03 November 2007

[334] Messaging Anti-Abuse Working Group (2007) MAAWG Attacks BotNets with Walled Garden Best Practices to Protect Users. http://www.maawg.org/news/maawg071002. Accessed 03 November 2007

[335] Messaging Anti-Abuse Working Group (2008) Press Releases. http://www.maawg.org/news/. Accessed 10 August 2008

150

[336] Messaging Anti-Abuse Working Group (2008) MAAWG Calendar 2008. Upcoming Events. http://www.maawg.org/news/events/. Accessed 10 August 2008

[337] The Spamhaus Project (2007) About Spamhaus. http://www.spamhaus.org/organization/index.lasso. Accessed 03 November 2007

[338] The Spamhaus Project (2007) The Spamhaus Block List. http://www.spamhaus.org/sbl/index.lasso. Accessed 03 November 2007

[339] The Spamhaus Project. (2008) The Spamhaus Don't Route Or Peer List. http://www.spamhaus.org/drop/index.lasso. Accessed 03 November 2007

[340] The Spamhaus Project (2007) Exploits Block List. http://www.spamhaus.org/xbl/index.lasso. Accessed 03 November 2007

[341] The Spamhaus Project (2007) The Policy Block List. http://www.spamhaus.org/pbl/index.lasso. Accessed 03 November 2007

[342] The Spamhaus Project (2007) zen.spamhaus.org. http://www.spamhaus.org/zen/. Accessed 03 November 2007

[343] The Spamhaus Project (2007) The ROKSO List. http://www.spamhaus.org/rokso/index.lasso. Accessed 03 November 2007

[344] StopSpamAlliance.org (2007) About. http://stopspamalliance.org/?page_id=2. Accessed 03 November 2007

[345] StopSpamAlliance.org (2007) About. http://stopspamalliance.org/?page_id=2. Accessed 03 November 2007

[346] StopSpamAlliance.org (2008) StopSpamAlliance.org. http://stopspamalliance.org/. Accessed 10 August 2008

[347] SpotSpam (2005) Goals – Enforcement and Threat Assessment. http://www.spotspam.net/goals.html. Accessed 10 August 2008

[348] SpotSpam (2005) EU project. http://www.spotspam.net/eu_project.html. Accessed 10 August 2008

[349] SpotSpam (2005) Project Description. http://www.spotspam.net/project_desc.html. Accessed 10 August 2008

[350] SpotSpam (2005) News. http://www.spotspam.net/news.html. Accessed 10 August 2008

[351] Rechtsanwalt T (2007) SpotSpam: The European Spambox Project. http://www.eco.de/dokumente/2a_Eco_Spotspam_TRickert_5dask2007.pdf. Accessed 10 August 2008

[352] Anti-Phishing Working Group (2008) APWG. http://www.antiphishing.org/. Accessed 03 November 2007

[353] Anti-Phishing Working Group (2008) APWG. http://www.antiphishing.org/. Accessed 03 November 2007

[354] Anti-Phishing Working Group (2008) Counter eCrime Operations Summit II. http://www.antiphishing.org/events/2008_operationsSummit.html. Accessed 10 August 2008

[355] Anti-Phishing Working Group (2008) APWG eCrime Researchers Summit. http://www.antiphishing.org/ecrimeresearch/index.html. Accessed 10 August 2008

[356] Anti-Spyware Coalition (2008) About ASC. http://www.antispywarecoalition.org/about. Accessed 03 November 2007

[357] Anti-Spyware Coalition (2008) Documents. http://www.antispywarecoalition.org/documents/index.htm. Accessed 10 August 2008

[358] Anti-Spyware Coalition (2006) Anti-Spyware Coalition Public Workshop: Defining the Problem, Developing Solutions. Events. http://www.antispywarecoalition.org/events/feb2006agenda.htm. Accessed 10 August 2008

[359] Anti-Spyware Coalition (2008) Events. http://www.antispywarecoalition.org/events/index.htm. Accessed 11 August 2008

[360] McCloskey P (2007) FBI, Carnegie Mellon Identify 1 MM Botnet Nodes. Campus Technology. http://campustechnology.com/articles/49053/. Accessed 11 August 2008

[361] Organisation for Economic Co-operation and Development (2007) Who is behind malware, their capabilities and activities? 35th Meeting of APEC Telecommunications and Information Working Group (APEC Tel 35). http://www.oecd.org/dataoecd/34/35/38653130.pdf. Accessed 11 August 2008

[362] Charney S (2005) Combating Cybercrime: A Public-Private Strategy in the Digital Environment. 11th United Nations Congress on Crime Prevention and Criminal Justice. http://www.nwacc.org/programs/conf05/UNCrimeCongressPaper.doc. Accessed 11 August 2008

[363] U.S. Department of Justice (2007) Prepared Remarks of Attorney General Alberto R. Gonzales at the Technet Intellectual Property Event. http://www.usdoj.gov/archive/ag/speeches/2007/ag_speech_070627.html. Accessed 11 August 2008

[364] U.S. Federal Bureau of Investigation (2007) OPERATION: BOT ROAST: 'Bot-herders' Charged as Part of Initiative. Headline Archives. http://www.fbi.gov/page2/june07/botnet061307.htm. Accessed 11 August 2008

[365] U.S. Federal Bureau of Investigation (2007) Over 1 Million Potential Victims of Botnet Cyber Crime. Press Release. http://www.fbi.gov/pressrel/pressrel07/botnet061307.htm. Accessed 11 August 2008

[366] NetworkWorld (2007) FBI 'Bot Roast II': 1 million infected PCs, $20 million in losses and 8 indictments. http://www.networkworld.com/community/node/22413. Accessed 11 August 2008

152

367   iDefense   Labs   (2008)   Conferences   and   Trade   Shows. http://labs.idefense.com/events/industry.php. Accessed 11 August 2008

368 International Secure Systems Lab (2008) News. http://www.iseclab.org/. Accessed 11 August 2008

369 Computer Emergency Response Team (2008) Meet CERT. Software Engineering Institute, Carnegie Mellon University. http://www.cert.org/meet_cert/. Accessed 17 November 2007

370 Morel B, Tagert D (2007) Information Security Teams for Developing Countries. Department of Engineering and Public Policy, Carnegie Mellon University. Pittsburgh, Pennsylvania

371 Forum of Incident Response and Security Teams (2008) FIRST Members. http://www.first.org/members/map/index.html. Accessed 27 August 2008

372 Forum of Incident Response and Security Teams (2007) Guidelines for the Membership Application Process. http://www.first.org/members/application/index.html. Accessed 03 November 2007

373 Forum of Incident Response and Security Teams (2006) FIRST Best Practice Guide Library (BPGL). http://www.first.org/resources/guides/. Accessed 21 July 2007

374 Morel B, Tagert D (2007) Information Security Teams for Developing Countries. Department of Engineering and Public Policy, Carnegie Mellon University. Pittsburgh, Pennsylvania

375   Authentication   and   Online   Trust   Alliance   (2008)   About   Us. http://www.aotalliance.org/about/. Accessed 11 August 2008

376 Authentication and Online Trust Alliance (2008) Working Committees & Chairs. http://www.aotalliance.org/about/commitees.html. Accessed 11 August 2008

377 Authentication and Online Trust Alliance (2008) Email Authentication Resources & Compliance Reports. http://www.aotalliance.org/resources/authentication/index.html. Accessed 11 August 2008

378 Authentication and Online Trust Alliance (2008) Press Release: AOTA Forms Online Trust Ecosystem to Combat Internet Abuse. http://www.aotalliance.org/news/releases/AOTAboard-1-8-08.html. Accessed 11 August 2008

379 Authentication and Online Trust Alliance (2008) Press Release: AOTA Urges Adoption of Extended Validation SSL Certificates. http://www.aotalliance.org/news/releases/AOTA. Accessed 11 August 2008

380 Authentication and Online Trust Alliance (2008) Extended Validation (EV) Secure Sockets Layer (SSL) Certificate Resources. http://www.aotalliance.org/resources/EV/index.html. Accessed 11 August 2008

381 Authentication and Online Trust Alliance (2008) Press Release: AOTA Urges Adoption of Extended Validation SSL Certificates. http://www.aotalliance.org/news/releases/AOTA. Accessed 11 August 2008

382 Authentication and Online Trust Alliance (2008) State of Email Authentication and the Internet Trust Ecosystem. http://www.aotalliance.org/resources/authentication/2008%20AOTA%20Authentication%20Report%2001-30.pdf. Accessed 11 August 2008

383 Authentication and Online Trust Alliance (2008) Agenda - AOTA Summit 2008 – Reaching the Tipping Point: Future of Online Trust. http://www.aotalliance.org/summit2008/program.html. Accessed 11 August 2008

384 Authentication and Online Trust Alliance (2008) AOTA Email Deliverability & Trust Academy. http://www.aotalliance.org/summit2008/academy.html. Accessed 11 August 2008

385 Global Information Infrastructure Commission (2007) The GIIC Mission Statement. http://www.giic.org/about/. Accessed 11 August 2008

386 World Information Technology and Services Alliance (1998) A Global Action Plan for Electronic Business: Prepared by Business with Recommendations for Governments. http://www.witsa.org/papers/globecom.htm. Accessed 11 August 2008

387 World Information Technology and Services Alliance (1998) A Global Action Plan for Electronic Business: Prepared by Business with Recommendations for Governments. http://www.witsa.org/papers/globecom.htm. Accessed 11 August 2008

388 International Chamber of Commerce (2008) What is ICC? http://www.iccwbo.org/id93/index.html. Accessed 22 July 2007

389 International Chamber of Commerce (2007) ICC Commission on E-Business, IT and Telecoms (EBITT). E-business, IT & Telecoms, Policy and Business Practices. http://www.iccwbo.org/policy/ebitt/id2340/index.html. Accessed 22 July 2007

390 International Chamber of Commerce (2007) ICC Commission on E-Business, IT and Telecoms (EBITT). E-business, IT & Telecoms, Policy and Business Practices. http://www.iccwbo.org/policy/ebitt/id2340/index.html. Accessed 22 July 2007

391 International Chamber of Commerce (2003) ICC recommendations to signatory states to contemplate when implementing the Council of Europe Convention on Cybercrime and its First Additional Protocol. Task Force on Cybercrime/Cyber Security, Commission on E-Business, IT & Telecoms. http://www.iccwbo.org/home/statements_rules/statements/2003/4%20ICC%20key%20recommendations%20to%20signatory%20states.pdf. Accessed 11 August 2008

392 International Chamber of Commerce (2003) Information security assurance for executives. Business and Industry Advisory Committee to the OECD (BIAC). http://www.iccwbo.org/uploadedFiles/ICC. Accessed 11 August 2008

393 International Chamber of Commerce (2004) ICC policy statement on 'spam' and unsolicited commercial electronic messages. Policy Statement. http://www.iccwbo.org/home/e_business/policy/373-22_114_spam.pdf. Accessed 11 August 2008

394 International Chamber of Commerce (2006) ICC framework for consultation and drafting of Information Compliance obligations. Policy Statement.

154

http://www.iccwbo.org/uploadedFiles/ICC/policy/e-business/pages/373-472_information_compliance.pdf. Accessed 11 August 2008

[395] International Federation for Information Processing (2007) About us. http://www.ifip.org/index.php?option=com_content&task=view&id=56&Itemid=110. Accessed 05 December 2007

[396] International Federation for Information Processing (2006) Aim & Scope. IFIP TC11. http://www.tc11.uni-frankfurt.de/aims_scope.htm. Accessed 05 December 2007

[397] International Federation for Information Processing (2007) Working Groups. IFIP TC11. http://www.tc11.uni-frankfurt.de/WG/index.htm. Accessed 05 December 2007

[398] International Federation for Information Processing (2008) The IFIP World Computer Congress - WCC 2008. http://www.wcc2008.org/site/congress.php. Accessed 05 December 2007

[399] International Federation for Information Processing (2007) 1st Annual IFIP WG 11.10 International Conference on Critical Infrastructure Protection. Call for Papers. http://www.tc11.uni-frankfurt.de/CONF/2007/WG11-10CallForPapers2007.pdf. Accessed 11 August 2008

[400] International Federation for Information Processing (2007) Introduction. 22nd IFIP TC-11 International Information Security Conference. http://www.sbs.co.za/ifipsec2007/ifipsec2007_INTRO.htm. Accessed 11 August 2008

[401] Open Information Systems Security Group (2007) About OISSG. http://www.oissg.org/about-oissg.html. Accessed 30 November 2007

[402] Open Information Systems Security Group (2007) Local Chapters. http://www.oissg.org/local-chapters.html. Accessed 30 November 2007

[403] Open Information Systems Security Group (2007) Overview. http://www.oissg.org/overview-3.html. Accessed 30 November 2007

[404] Open Information Systems Security Group (2007) Vulnerability Research. http://www.oissg.org/vulnerability-research.html. Accessed 30 November 2007

[405] Open Information Systems Security Group (2007) Vulnerability Disclosure Policy. http://www.oissg.org/vdp.html. Accessed 30 November 2007

[406] Open Information Systems Security Group (2007) Password Security Research. http://www.oissg.org/password-security-research.html. Accessed 30 November 2007

[407] Open Information Systems Security Group (2007) Business Continuity Planning and Disaster Recovery. http://www.oissg.org/business-continuity-planning-and-disaster-recovery.html. Accessed 30 November 2007

[408] Open Information Systems Security Group (2007) IRM. http://www.oissg.org/irm.html. Accessed 30 November 2007

[409] Open Information Systems Security Group (2007) Metacoretex-NG. http://www.oissg.org/invisible/metacoretex-ng.html. Accessed 30 November 2007

410   Open   Information   Systems   Security   Group   (2007)   Bookmarks   List.
http://www.oissg.org/links/list/onecat/Root/0.html. Accessed 30 November 2007

411   Open   Information   Systems   Security   Group   (2007)   Welcome   to   OISSG.
http://www.oissg.org/. Accessed 30 November 2007

412 Open Information Systems Security Group (2007) Information Systems Security Assessment
Framework   (ISSAF).   http://www.oissg.org/information-systems-security-assessment-
framework-issaf.html. Accessed 30 November 2007

413 Open Information Systems Security Group (2007) Computer Crime Investigation Framework
(CCIF). http://www.oissg.org/computer-crime-investigation-framework-ccif.html. Accessed
30 November 2007

414   Open   Information   Systems   Security   Group   (2007)   Security   Essentials   Framework.
http://www.oissg.org/security-essentials-framework-sef.html. Accessed 30 November 2007

415   Open   Information   Systems   Security   Group   (2007)   Capture   the   Flag   (CTF).
http://www.oissg.org/capture-the-flag-ctf.html. Accessed 30 November 2007

416 Open Information Systems Security Group (2008) ISSAF Free Conferences: Briefings.
http://www.oissg.org/briefings/index.php. Accessed 11 August 2008

417   The   Society   of   the   Policing   of   Cyberspace   (2007)   Welcome.
http://www.polcyb.org/index.html. Accessed 11 August 2008

418   The   Society   of   the   Policing   of   Cyberspace   (2007)   Our   Vision.
http://www.polcyb.org/vision.html. Accessed 11 August 2008

419 The Society of the Policing of Cyberspace (2008) POLCYB Quarterly Meeting Presentation.
POLCYB Quarterly Meeting. http://www.polcyb.org/Events/qm_Mar2008.html. Accessed 11
August 2008

420 The Society of the Policing of Cyberspace (2007) POLCYB Annual General Meeting Presentation.   POLCYB   Annual   General   Meeting.
http://www.polcyb.org/Events/annualgeneralmeeting.html. Accessed 11 August 2008

421 The Society of the Policing of Cyberspace (2007) POLCYB International Summit 2007.
http://www.polcyb.org/summit_2007/summit_2007.html. Accessed 11 August 2008

422 The Society of the Policing of Cyberspace (2007) Conference Themes and Topics. POLCYB
International Summit 2007. http://www.polcyb.org/summit_2007/topics.html. Accessed 11
August 2008

423 The Society of the Policing of Cyberspace (2008) POLCYB International Summit 2008.
http://www.polcyb.org/summit_2008/summit_2008.html. Accessed 11 August 2008

424 The Society of the Policing of Cyberspace (2008) POLCYB International Conference 2008.
http://www.polcyb.org/conf_2008/conf_2008.html. Accessed 11 August 2008

156

[425] The SANS Institute (2008) About SANS. http://www.sans.org/about/sans.php. Accessed 27 August 2008

[426] The SANS Institute (2008) SANS Course List & SANS Training by Course. http://www.sans.org/training/courses.php. Accessed 27 August 2008

[427] The SANS Institute (2008) Global Information Assurance Certification. http://www.giac.org/. Accessed 27 August 2008

[428] The SANS Institute (2007) SANS Cyber Defense Initiative 2007. http://www.sans.org/cdi07/. Accessed 28 August 2008

[429] The SANS Institute (2008) SANSFIRE 2008. https://www.sans.org/sansfire08/. Accessed 28 August 2008

[430] The SANS Institute (2008) SANS WhatWorks Summit in Forensics and Incident Response. http://www.sans.org/forensics08_summit/. Accessed 28 August 2008

[431] The SANS Institute (2008) SANS Free Resources. http://www.sans.org/free_resources.php. Accessed 27 August 2008

[432] The SANS Institute (2008) About the Internet Storm Center. http://isc.sans.org/about.html. Accessed 27 August 2008

[433] The SANS Institute (2008) What is the Software Security Institute? http://www.sans-ssi.org/. Accessed 28 August 2008

[434] The SANS Institute (2008) Education Leaders Unite. http://www.sans.org/press/leaders_unite.php. Accessed 28 August 2008

[435] The SANS Institute (2008) SANS Announces $1 Million Grant to Expand Cyber Security Capacity of Developing Countries "We Are All In This Together." http://www.sans.org/press/impact.php. Accessed 28 August 2008

[436] World Information Technology and Services Alliance (2007) About WITSA. http://www.witsa.org/about/index.htm. Accessed 02 December 2007

[437] World Information Technology and Services Alliance (2005) Bylaws. http://www.witsa.org/about/Bylaws20050913.pdf. Accessed 11 August 2008

[438] World Information Technology and Services Alliance (2008) WITSA Task Forces. http://www.witsa.org/about/tforces.htm. Accessed 11 August 2008

[439] World Information Technology and Services Alliance (2007) Global Public Policy Conference (GPPC): 4-6 November 2007. http://www.gppc2007.com/. Accessed 03 December 2007

[440] World Information Technology and Services Alliance (2007) Plenary Session Agenda: Information Security and Privacy. Global Public Policy Conference 2007. http://www.gppc2007.com/session-5.htm. Accessed 12 August 2008

[441] Wright A (2007) Bermuda to host 2009 global IT conference. The Royal Gazette. http://www.witsa.org/gppc2009/TheRoyalGazette_article.pdf. Accessed 11 August 2008

[442] World Information Technology and Services Alliance (2007) About WCIT 2008. 16th World Congress on Information and Technology. http://www.wcit2008.org/About/default.aspx. Accessed 11 August 2008

[443] World Information Technology and Services Alliance (2008) Program. 16th World Congress on Information Technology. http://www.wcit2008.org/program.htm. Accessed 12 August 2008

[444] World Information Technology and Services Alliance (1998) Government and Law Enforcement Access to Transmitted Information in the Digital Environment. WITSA Statement. http://www.witsa.org/papers/lawenf.pdf. Accessed 11 August 2008

[445] World Information Technology and Services Alliance (1999) Statement - Critical Information Protection (CIP): A Framework for Government/Industry Dialogue. http://www.witsa.org/papers/cip.htm. Accessed 11 August 2008

[446] World Information Technology and Services Alliance (2000) International IT Industry Survey: Cyber Security a Top Priority. http://www.witsa.org/papers/CipSurv.pdf. Accessed 11 August 2008

[447] World Information Technology and Services Alliance (2000) Cyber Crime... and Punishment? Archaic Laws Threaten Global Information. McConnell International. http://www.witsa.org/papers/McConnell-cybercrime.pdf. Accessed 11 August 2008

[448] World Information Technology and Services Alliance (2000) G-8 Heads of Delegation. WITSA Secretariat. http://www.witsa.org/press/G8ltr.pdf. Accessed 11 August 2008

[449] World Information Technology and Services Alliance (2000) Global High Tech Industry Group Voices Concerns Over Draft Cyber-Crime Convention. http://www.witsa.org/press/COEpr.pdf. Accessed 11 August 2008

[450] World Information Technology and Services Alliance (2004) Background Paper on Traffic Data Requirements and Cooperation with Law Enforcement Authorities. http://www.witsa.org/papers/DataRetention-final.pdf. Accessed 11 August 2008

[451] World Information Technology and Services Alliance (2006) Information Security: Building a Sustainable Program. http://www.witsa.org/ITMA/Final_InfoSec_Toolkit.doc. Accessed 11 August 2008

[452] World Information Technology and Services Alliance (2006) Key Findings: WITSA eGovernment Survey. http://www.witsa.org/athens06/WITSA_EGovReportOct2006.pdf. Accessed 11 August 2008

[453] World Information Technology and Services Alliance (2002) Statement on Information Security. http://www.witsa.org/papers/infosec2002.pdf. Accessed 11 August 2008

[454] World Information Technology and Services Alliance (2005) Statement on Information Security. http://www.witsa.org/papers/WITSA. Accessed 11 August 2008

[455] World Information Technology and Services Alliance (2007) Views of the World Information Technology and Services Alliance (WITSA) on the Internet Governance Forum. http://www.witsa.org/igf/WITSAIGF2007.doc. Accessed 11 August 2008

[456] World Information Technology and Services Alliance (2008) The GIP Advisory Committee to WITSA. Global Internet Project. http://www.witsa.org/gip/about/. Accessed 11 August 2008

[457] World Information Technology and Services Alliance (2008) GIP – Security. Global Internet Project. http://www.witsa.org/gip/security/. Accessed 11 August 2008

[458] 3rd Generation Partnership Project (2008) About 3GPP. http://www.3gpp.org/About/about.htm. Accessed 12 August 2008

[459] 3rd Generation Partnership Project (2007) TSG SA WG3 – Overview. http://www.3gpp.org/tb/SA/SA3/SA3.htm. Accessed 12 August 2008

[460] 3rd Generation Partnership Project (2002) Algorithms. http://www.3gpp.org/tb/Other/algorithms.htm. Accessed 12 August 2008

[461] 3rd Generation Partnership Project (2008) 3GPP Specifications for group: S3 (showing rapporteur). http://www.3gpp.org/ftp/Specs/html-info/TSG-WG--S3.htm. Accessed 12 August 2008

[462] 3rd Generation Partnership Project (2008) WG3_Security. http://www.3gpp.org/ftp/tsg_sa/WG3_Security/. Accessed 12 August 2008

[463] 3rd Generation Partnership Project (2008) Active 3GPP Work Items for group: S3. 3GPP Work Items per TSG/WG. http://www.3gpp.org/ftp/Specs/html-info/TSG-WG--s3--wis.htm. Accessed 12 August 2008

[464] 3rd Generation Partnership Project (2008) 3GPP meetings for group: S3. http://www.3gpp.org/ftp/Specs/html-info/Meetings-S3.htm. Accessed 12 August 2008

[465] Central and Eastern European Networking Association (2008) CEENet. http://www.ceenet.org/. Accessed 11 August 2008

[466] Central and Eastern European Networking Association (2000) Session 6: Security and Accessibility. The Preliminary Program of The Second CEENet Workshop on Network Management/NATO Advanced Networking Workshop. http://www.ohridanw2000.marnet.mk/programmeD.html#session6. Accessed 11 August 2008

[467] Gajewski J (2005) Training and funding for security related projects. Central and Eastern European Networking Association. http://www.ceenet.org/presentations/CEENet. Accessed 11 August 2008

[468] Cooperative Association for Internet Data Analysis (2008) Frequently Asked Questions About CAIDA. http://www.caida.org/home/about/faq.xml. Accessed 18 August 2008

[469] Cooperative Association for Internet Data Analysis (2007) Research - Security. http://www.caida.org/research/security/. Accessed 18 August 2008

[470] Cooperative Association for Internet Data Analysis (2008) Presentations by CAIDA. http://www.caida.org/publications/presentations/bytopic/index.xml#security. Accessed 20 August 2008

[471] Cooperative Association for Internet Data Analysis (2008) Presentations by CAIDA. http://www.caida.org/publications/presentations/bytopic/index.xml#security. Accessed 20 August 2008

[472] American Registry for Internet Numbers (2008) ARIN Report May 2008. http://www.arin.net/newsletter/2008_May.pdf. Accessed 20 August 2008

[473] The GSM Association (2008) About the GSM Association. GSM World. http://www.gsmworld.com/about/index.shtml. Accessed 11 August 2008

[474] The GSM Association (2005) Mobile Application Security: Background. Deliverables. Recommendations. MAS Gen Doc 002. http://www.gsmworld.com/using/security/gsma_mas_final_summary_v1.pdf. Accessed 11 August 2008

[475] The GSM Association (2008) Mobile Application Security. GSM World. http://www.gsmworld.com/using/security/mobile_application.shtml. Accessed 11 August 2008

[476] The GSM Association (2008) GSM Security Algorithms. GSM World. http://www.gsmworld.com/using/algorithms/index.shtml. Accessed 11 August 2008

[477] The GSM Association (2008) Security Accreditation Scheme. GSM World. http://www.gsmworld.com/using/sas/index.shtml. Accessed 11 August 2008

[478] The GSM Association (2008) GSMA Certified Fraud Training Programme. GSM World. http://www.gsmworld.com/fraudtraining/index.shtml. Accessed 11 August 2008

[479] The GSM Association (2008) About the programme. GSM World. http://www.gsmworld.com/fraudtraining/about.shtml. Accessed 11 August 2008

[480] The GSM Association (2008) Upcoming Courses. GSM World. http://www.gsmworld.com/fraudtraining/courses.shtml. Accessed 11 August 2008

[481] The GSM Association (2008) Security Advice for Mobile Phone Users. GSM World. http://www.gsmworld.com/using/security/advice.shtml. Accessed 11 August 2008

[482] IEEE (2008) History of the IEEE. http://www.ieee.org/web/aboutus/history/index.html. Accessed 20 August 2008

[483] IEEE (2007) About IEEE. http://www.ieee.org/web/aboutus/home/index.html. Accessed 20 August 2008

[484] IEEE (2008) IEEE Symposium on Security and Privacy. http://www.ieee-security.org/TC/SP-Index.html. Accessed 20 August 2008

[485] IEEE (2008) 2008 IEEE Symposium on Security and Privacy. http://www.ieee-security.org/TC/SP2008/oakland08.html. Accessed 20 August 2008

[486] Department of Computer Science, University of Virginia (2008) IEEE Symposium on Security and Privacy. http://oakland09.cs.virginia.edu/. Accessed 20 August 2008

[487] IEEE (2008) Computer Security Foundations Symposium. http://www.ieee-security.org/CSFWweb/index.html. Accessed 20 August 2008

[488] CyLab, Carnegie Mellon University (2008) 21st IEEE Computer Security Foundations Symposium. http://www.cylab.cmu.edu/CSF2008/. Accessed 20 August 2008

[489] IEEE (2008) IEEE Security & Privacy: About Us. http://www.computer.org/portal/pages/security/content/about.html. Accessed 20 August 2008

[490] IEEE (2008) Cipher. http://www.ieee-security.org/cipher.html. Accessed 20 August 2008

[491] International Organization for Standardization (2008) About ISO. http://www.iso.org/iso/about.htm. Accessed 11 August 2008

[492] International Organization for Standardization (2008) ISO/IEC security standards. International standardization on security. ISO/IEC/ITU. http://www.iso.org/iso/iss_international-security-standards.htm. Accessed 11 August 2008

[493] International Organization for Standardization (2008) ITU security roadmap. International standardization on security. ISO/IEC/ITU. http://www.iso.org/iso/iss_itu-security-roadmap.htm. Accessed 11 August 2008

[494] International Organization for Standardization (2008) ISO Technical Committees. International standardization on security. ISO/IEC/ITU. http://www.iso.org/iso/iss_technical-committees.htm. Accessed 11 August 2008

[495] International Organization for Standardization (2007) SC 27 Business Plan October 2007 - September 2008. ISO/IEC JTC1/SC 27. ISO/IEC. http://isotc.iso.org/livelink/livelink/fetch/2000/2122/327993/327974/1057737/4752556/SC27 N6040_SC27_Business_Plan_2007-10_2008-09.pdf?nodeid=7240060&vernum=0. Accessed 11 August 2008

[496] International Organization for Standardization (2005) Final Report of ISO Advisory Group on Security. Document: ISO/IEC/TMB SAG N05. ISO/IEC. http://www.iso.org/iso/n05_final_report_ags.pdf. Accessed 11 August 2008

[497] International Organization for Standardization (2008) Report on the 5th meeting of the ISO/IEC/ITU-T Strategic Advisory Group on Security. Document: ISO/IEC/ITU-T SAG-S N112. ISO/IEC/ITU. http://www.iso.org/iso/n112_report_5thsag-s_mtg_geneva_23-24jan2008.pdf. Accessed 11 August 2008

[498] Internet Engineering Task Force (2007) Overview of the IETF. http://www.ietf.org/overview.html. Accessed 28 November 2007

[499] Alvestrand H (2004) A Mission Statement for the IETF. Network Working Group, The Internet Society. http://www.ietf.org/rfc/rfc3935.txt. Accessed 11 August 2008

[500] Hoffman P (2006) The Tao of IETF: A Novice's Guide to the Internet Engineering Task Force. Network Working Group, The Internet Society. http://www.ietf.org/tao.html. Accessed 11 August 2008

[501] Internet Engineering Task Force (2007) Overview of the IETF. http://www.ietf.org/overview.html. Accessed 28 November 2007

[502] Internet Engineering Task Force (2008) The IETF Security Area. Sec Area Wiki. http://www3.tools.ietf.org/area/sec/trac/wiki. Accessed 11 August 2008

[503] Internet Engineering Task Force (2007) Overview of the IETF. http://www.ietf.org/overview.html. Accessed 28 November 2007

[504] Internet Research Task Force (2006) IRTF. http://www.irtf.org/. Accessed 20 August 2008

[505] Internet Research Task Force (2007) Anti-Spam Research Group. http://asrg.sp.am/. Accessed 20 August 2008

[506] Internet Research Task Force (2002) Crypto Forum Research Group. http://www.irtf.org/rg/cfrg/#about-cfrg. Accessed 20 August 2008

[507] Internet Research Task Force (2007) IP Mobility Optimizations (Mob Opts). http://people.nokia.net/%7Erajeev/mobopts/index.html. Accessed 20 August 2008

[508] Internet Research Task Force (2005) IRTF Peer-to-Peer Research Group. http://www.irtf.org/charter.php?gtype=rg&group=p2prg. Accessed 20 August 2008

[509] The Internet Society (2007) Introduction to ISOC. http://www.isoc.org/isoc/. Accessed 03 November 2007

[510] The Internet Society (2008) Key Issues. Public Policy. http://www.isoc.org/pubpolpillar/issues/security.shtml. Accessed 11 August 2008

[511] The Internet Society (2008) Initiatives for 2008-2010. About The Internet Society. http://www.isoc.org/isoc/mission/initiative/. Accessed 11 August 2008

[512] The Internet Society (2007) Network and Distributed System Security Symposium (NDSS). Conferences and Events. http://www.isoc.org/isoc/conferences/ndss/. Accessed 03 November 2007

[513] The Internet Society (2007) The 14th Annual Network & Distributed System Security Symposium. NDSS Symposium 2007. http://www.isoc.org/isoc/conferences/ndss/07/. Accessed 11 August 2008

[514] The Internet Society (2008) The 15th Annual Network & Distributed System Security Symposium. NDSS Symposium 2008. http://www.isoc.org/isoc/conferences/ndss/08/. Accessed 11 August 2008

[515] The Internet Society (2008) INET Conferences. Conferences and Events. http://www.isoc.org/isoc/conferences/. Accessed 11 August 2008

162

[516] The Internet Society (2008) Security Expert Initiative. Public Policy. http://www.isoc.org/pubpolpillar/seinit.shtml. Accessed 11 August 2008

[517] The Internet Society (2008) Call for Participation: Trust and the Future of the Internet. About The Internet Society. http://www.isoc.org/isoc/general/trustees/headlines/20070809.shtml. Accessed 11 August 2008

[518] Bommelaer C (2006) ISOC's participation in the ITU Telecom World 2006 as chair of the Spam Workshop. The Internet Society. http://www.isoc.org/pubpolpillar/docs/ISOC_chairs_spam_session.pdf. Accessed 11 August 2008

[519] Organization for the Advancement of Structured Information Standards (2008) About OASIS. http://www.oasis-open.org/who/. Accessed 20 August 2008

[520] Organization for the Advancement of Structured Information Standards (2008) OASIS Events. http://www.oasis-open.org/events/. Accessed 20 August 2008

[521] Organization for the Advancement of Structured Information Standards (2008) OASIS Committees by Category: Security. http://www.oasis-open.org/committees/tc_cat.php?cat=security. Accessed 20 August 2008

[522] Organization for the Advancement of Structured Information Standards (2008) OASIS Committees by Category: Security. http://www.oasis-open.org/committees/tc_cat.php?cat=security. Accessed 20 August 2008

[523] Organization for the Advancement of Structured Information Standards (2008) Open Standards Forum 2008: Security Challenges for the Information Society. http://events.oasis-open.org/home/forum/2008. Accessed 20 August 2008

[524] Organization for the Advancement of Structured Information Standards (2008) About the Forum. http://events.oasis-open.org/home/forum/2008/about. Accessed 20 August 2008

[525] The Trans-European Research and Education Networking Association (2007) Welcome to TERENA. http://www.terena.org/. Accessed 28 November 2007

[526] The Trans-European Research and Education Networking Association (2007) About TERENA. http://www.terena.org/about/. Accessed 28 November 2007

[527] The Trans-European Research and Education Networking Association (2007) TERENA Technical Programme. http://www.terena.org/about/tech/. Accessed 28 November 2007

[528] The Trans-European Research and Education Networking Association (2007) Authentication and Authorization. http://www.terena.org/activities/index.php?action=set_filters&filters[topic_id]=3. Accessed 28 November 2007

[529] The Trans-European Research and Education Networking Association (2007) Authentication and Authorization. http://www.terena.org/activities/index.php?action=set_filters&filters[topic_id]=3. Accessed 28 November 2007

[530] World Wide Web Consortium (2007) About the World Wide Web Consortium (W3C). http://www.w3.org/Consortium/Overview.html. Accessed 20 August 2008

[531] World Wide Web Consortium (2008) Security Activity Statement. http://www.w3.org/Security/Activity. Accessed 20 August 2008

[532] World Wide Web Consortium (2008) Web Security Context Working Group. http://www.w3.org/2006/WSC/. Accessed 20 August 2008

[533] World Wide Web Consortium (2008) XML Signature Syntax and Processing (Second Edition). http://www.w3.org/TR/2008/REC-xmldsig-core-20080610/. Accessed 20 August 2008

[534] World Wide Web Consortium (2008) Security Activity Statement. http://www.w3.org/Security/Activity. Accessed 20 August 2008

[535] World Wide Web Consortium (2008) W3C Security Home. http://www.w3.org/Security/. Accessed 20 August 2008

[536] Nain D, Donaghy N, Goodman S (2008) The International Landscape of Cyber Security. In: Straub D, Goodman S, Baskerville R (ed) Information Security: Policy, Processes, and Practices. M.E.Sharpe, New York

[537] Forum of Incident Response and Security Teams (2008) FIRST Members. http://www.first.org/members/map/index.html. Accessed 27 August 2008

[538] Nain D, Donaghy N, Goodman S (2008) The International Landscape of Cyber Security. In: Straub D, Goodman S, Baskerville R (ed) Information Security: Policy, Processes, and Practices. M.E.Sharpe, New York

Printed in the United States of America